Vocabulary for Success

COURSE IV

HAROLD LEVINE
Chairman Emeritus of English,
Benjamin Cardozo High School, New York

NORMAN LEVINE
Associate Professor of English,
City College of the City University of New York

ROBERT T. LEVINE
Professor of English,
North Carolina A & T State University

STEVEN L. STERN
Writer of educational materials
for children and adults

AMSCO

AMSCO SCHOOL PUBLICATIONS, INC.
315 Hudson Street / New York, N.Y. 10013

Vocabulary books by the authors

Vocabulary and Composition Through Pleasurable Reading,
Books I–IV
Vocabulary for Enjoyment, Books I–III
Vocabulary for the High School Student, Books A, B
Vocabulary for the High School Student
Vocabulary for the College-Bound Student
The Joy of Vocabulary
Vocabulary for Success, Courses I–IV

Cover Design: Meghan J. Shupe
Composition: Brad Walrod/High Text Graphics, Inc.

Please visit our Web site at:
www.amscopub.com

When ordering this book, please specify
either **R 014 P** or VOCABULARY FOR SUCCESS, COURSE IV

ISBN 1-56765-132-1
NYC Item 56765-132-0

Printed in the United States of America
1 2 3 4 5 6   11 10 09 08 07 06

To the Student

Course IV, like its predecessors in the *Vocabulary for Success* series, teaches not only words but also skills—especially the skills of close reading, critical thinking, and concise writing.

Each time you meet a lesson word in this book, you will be called upon to complete a sentence—not with the lesson word but with some other missing word. This, though you may not think so at first, requires close reading and critical thinking. Try to do what you are asked to do on page 1, and see if you don't agree. Then, for an example of a different way in which the book teaches these same skills, see pages 44–45.

Concise writing is still another skill you will be learning in every lesson in this vocabulary book. The fastest way to learn what this skill is about is to turn now to the first concise writing exercise on page 9.

By the time you finish the book, you will have had hundreds of opportunities to perfect your reading, writing, and thinking skills and you also will have learned many hundreds of useful words that belong in a well-educated person's vocabulary. Take a minute now to skim the Vocabulary Index, beginning on page 154.

You will find ample provision for review within each regular lesson. Note, too, that after every fourth lesson is a unit review.

Analogy questions have been included at the end of each unit, in part because they help with the review of lesson words and their synonyms, but more importantly because they stimulate critical thinking, a principal concern of this book.

The Authors

Contents

LESSON 1

Lesson Preview

Some of the words that you will encounter on pages 1–3 and 4–5 of this lesson appear in bold type in the following poem. Read the poem, and on a separate sheet of paper, answer the questions that follow.

> The ghost appeared inside my room—
> An **apparition** not too frightful—
> A **diffident** little fellow,
> Who proved to be most delightful.
>
> He had a **penchant** for telling jokes,
> And his **banter** was really quite funny.
> Not an **odious** spirit at all,
> But a personality rather sunny.

What is this poem about? Why wasn't the narrator scared of the ghost?

 LESSON WORDS 1–10: Pronounce the word, spell it, study its meanings, and finish the sentence that follows it. See 1 below.

---

adept (*adj.*)   thoroughly skilled; **proficient**; **expert**
ə-'dept

  1. Someone with (limited, substantial) __substantial__ driving experience is likely to be *adept* at operating a motor vehicle.

apparition (*n.*)   ghostly figure; **phantom**; **specter**
ˌa-pə-'ri-shən

  2. Scrooge reacted with (fright, glee) _____ when an *apparition* suddenly materialized in his bedroom.

1

banter (*n.*)   good-natured, playful joking or teasing; **jesting**;
'ban-tər   **repartee**

    3. Longtime (friends, enemies) _____ traded *banter*
       as they walked to school.

despondent (*adj.*)   feeling discouraged; **dejected**; **depressed**;
di-'spän-dənt   **despairing**

    4. Edwards was *despondent* when the head of the department
       (fired, promoted) _____ him.

diffident (*adj.*)   lacking confidence in oneself; **shy**; **timid**
'di-fə-dənt

    5. *Diffident* people generally try to (avoid, attract)
       _____ the attention of others.

discern (*v.*)   detect or recognize; **perceive**; **distinguish**; **see**
di-'sərn

    6. A (perceptive, foolish) _____ person can *discern*
       the difference between courage and recklessness.

enmity (*n.*)   feeling between enemies; **animosity**; **ill will**; **hatred**
'en-mə-tē

    7. The prolonged border dispute had (increased, decreased)
       _____ the *enmity* between the neighboring
       nations.

feign (*v.*)   put on a false appearance; make believe; **pretend**;
'fān   **simulate**

    8. Although she was (scared, fearless) _____, Jayne
       feigned courage as she stood in line for the roller coaster
       ride.

imperious (*adj.*)   marked by arrogance; **haughty**; **domineering**;
im-'pir-ē-əs   **overbearing**

    9. The photographer's *imperious* treatment of his assistants
       made him (difficult, pleasant) _____ to work for.

impromptu (*adj.*)   made or done without preparation; spur-of-the-
im-'präm(p)-,tü   moment; **extemporaneous**; **offhand**

10. Because of his (impulsive, cautious) _____ nature,
Joshua enjoys making *impromptu* speeches.

B **SENTENCE COMPLETION 1–10:** Enter the required lesson
   words, as in 1 below.

---

1. Even though George _____**feign**_____ed courage, the
   ___**apparition**___ frightened him.

2. During the campaign, the candidate had become quite
   _____ at holding _____ press conferences.

3. Emily grew _____ at the thought that her twin sister
   was moving away, already missing their daily _____.

4. Having a(n) _____ manner in victory can lead to
   _____ between competitors.

5. A _____ person may find it hard to _____ the
   pleasures of social situations.

C **VOCABULARY IN CONTEXT 1–10:** Read the paragraph,
   and on a separate sheet of paper, answer the questions
   that follow. Do not repeat any of the underlined words in
   your answers; use synonyms instead.

Be careful about the comments you make to others. Even
though someone may <u>feign</u> indifference to an unkind remark, he
or she may be suffering in silence. Some people are too <u>diffident</u>
to risk a confrontation, and they become quite <u>adept</u>
at hiding their true feelings. Nevertheless, these people may
become <u>despondent</u> when they recall how they have been
treated. So watch what you say, and try your best to <u>discern</u>
what effects your words have on others.

1. What is the main idea of this paragraph?

2. Do you agree or disagree with the writer's advice? Explain your answer.

D	**LESSON WORDS 11–20:** Pronounce the word, spell it, study its meanings, and finish the sentence that follows it.

---

incite (v.)   move to action; stir up; urge on; **instigate**; **provoke**;
in-'sīt   **rouse**

11. Police (arrested, praised) _____ the man when he tried to *incite* the protesters to riot.

insipid (adj.)   lacking in qualities that interest or stimulate; **dull**;
in-'si-pəd   **bland; colorless**

12. Book reviewers (disparaged, acclaimed) _____ the novelist for his *insipid* language and style.

mediate (v.)   bring about agreement by intervening between
'mē-dē-ăt   disputing persons or opposing sides; **intercede**;
     negotiate

13. It took lawyers several weeks to *mediate* a (settlement, tribute) _____ that management approved.

mortify (v.)   cause great embarrassment to; **humiliate**; **shame**
'mȯr-tə-fī

14. The children's (excellent, dreadful) _____ behavior in the restaurant *mortified* their parents.

odious (adj.)   causing hatred, disgust, or repugnance; **offensive**;
'ō-dē-əs   **detestable**

15. The speaker's *odious* comments (pleased, offended) _____ the audience.

penchant (*n.*)   strong inclination; **liking**; **leaning**
'pen-chənt

    16. Anyone with a *penchant* for home repair should (avoid, purchase) _____ power tools.

preclude (*v.*)   make impossible; **prevent**; **impede**
pri-'klüd

    17. We arrived at the party (early, late) _____ because the storm *precluded* our driving the most direct route.

restitution (*n.*)   making good of some loss, damage, or injury;
,res-tə-'tü-shən   **compensation**; **repayment**; **reparation**

    18. Since you are the one who (purchased, smashed) _____ the vase, it's only fair that you make *restitution*.

squalid (*adj.*)   characterized by filthiness and wretchedness, as
'skwä-ləd   from poverty or neglect; **foul**; **dirty**

    19. (Few, many) _____ families are willing to live in the city's most *squalid* apartment buildings.

veracity (*n.*)   adherence to the truth; **truthfulness**; **honesty**
və-'ra-sə-tē

    20. Because Jeff is well-known for his *veracity*, (no one, everyone) _____ doubts his account of events.

E   **SENTENCE COMPLETION 11–20:** Enter the required lesson words from D, above.

---

  1. The author's _____ comments during the radio interview _____**d** the membership committee's inviting him to join the writers' club.

  2. Security officials rushed to _____ the dispute for fear that rising tempers might _____ a riot.

3. When Jeremy visited the run-down old building, he was
_____**ed** that his cousin could live in such
_____ conditions.

4. Because of your _____ in explaining what happened,
we will not ask you to make _____ for the damage you
accidentally caused.

5. Although she has a(n) _____ for writing clever
metaphors, her lyrics are generally _____.

F   **VOCABULARY IN CONTEXT 11–20:** Read the paragraph,
and on a separate sheet of paper, answer the questions
that follow. Do not repeat any of the underlined words in
your answers; use synonyms instead.

Because Jordyn has always had a penchant for public speaking,
no one was surprised that she became an attorney. Her first
case involved a homeowner whose property had been damaged
by a careless driver. The homeowner wanted restitution, but
the driver—a rather odious individual—refused. Attempts to
mediate the dispute failed, so the case went to court. Jordyn
won, after calling into question the veracity of the driver's
account of events.

1. Paraphrase the paragraph.

2. Suppose you were the lawyer representing the driver, and you
discovered halfway through the trial that your client was lying.
Would you be mortified? Why or why not?

SYNONYMS: To avoid repetition, replace the boldfaced word with a synonym from the vocabulary list below. See 1 below.

proficient	phantom	shy	distinguish	haughty
dull	negotiate	detestable	dirty	truthfulness

1. Even though her diffidence made Lana feel uncomfortable in social situations, she found it hard to overcome her **diffident** nature.

1. _____**shy**_____

2. The **squalid** tenement was located on the south side of city, an area noted for its poverty and squalor.

2. _____

3. Although the prime minister thought of himself as a discerning judge of character, he could not **discern** his true allies from those who wanted only to share his power.

3. _____

4. If the mediators are unable to **mediate** a satisfactory agreement by midnight, workers will go out on strike.

4. _____

5. The queen's imperial bearing impressed her subjects, but her **imperious** manner irritated her siblings.

5. _____

6. A strange **apparition** appeared out of the dense fog and slowly approached us.

6. _____

7. Anyone who writes prose as **insipid** as this report can be expected to demonstrate the same insipidness in conversation.

7. _____

8. The lawyer doubted the **veracity** of the witness's testimony, but she did not have sufficient evidence to verify another explanation of events.

8. _____

9. Only the most **odious** criminals could
commit such odious crimes, and they
will be severely punished.   9. _____

10. Aliya is an **adept** basketball player
who handles the ball adeptly and
shoots with remarkable accuracy.   10. _____

H   **ANTONYMS:** In the blank space in each sentence below,
enter the word most nearly the antonym of the boldfaced
word. Choose your antonyms from the following list. See
1 below.

---

deceitfulness	fascinating	cheerful	goodwill	inept
clean	outgoing	organized	aversion	charming

1. It took many years, but eventually the **enmity** between the two
families gave way to understanding and ___**goodwill**___.

2. The Falcons, who had been so _____ at the start of the
game, became **despondent** as the opposing team's lead grew.

3. After years of hard work and careful saving, we were able to
move from our **squalid** little apartment into a(n) _____
and spacious house.

4. Carla is _____ at most sports, but she is an **adept**
chess player.

5. Although the meeting was supposedly **impromptu**, it seemed
suspiciously well _____.

6. The advice of a psychologist helped Max become less **diffident**
and more _____.

7. The speaker began with a rather **insipid** opening but then
became increasingly _____ as he continued.

8. Howard's _____ in the past made us doubt the **veracity** of his explanation.

9. The main character, who seems so _____ in the first
few chapters of the novel, proves to be an **odious** villain by the
end.

10. Ginny has a **penchant** for bold action, while her brother has
a(n) _____ to any sort of confrontation.

CONCISE WRITING: Express the thought of each sentence in NO MORE THAN FOUR WORDS. See 1 below.

1. People who are friendly often trade good-natured, playful joking with each other.

   Friends often exchange banter.

2. Ken is a person who lacks confidence in himself.

   _____

3. This essay is lacking in qualities that would interest or stimulate anyone reading it.

   _____

4. You have to make good for the damage that resulted from your actions.

   _____

5. The words that you spoke caused great embarrassment to me.

   _____

6. The conference was held with absolutely no advance preparation of any kind.

   _____

VOCABULARY SKILL BUILDER

Context Clues: Inferring the Meaning of Words

You can often determine the meaning of an unfamiliar word by thinking carefully about the context in which the word is used. _Context_ means the surrounding words, sentences, or even paragraphs.

When you use context clues to figure out a word's meaning, you are *making an inference*. That is, you are combining information from the context with your own knowledge and experience to reach a conclusion. Context clues can also help you decide which meaning is appropriate when you encounter a word that has multiple meanings.

> *Example:* As Julien carried his cafeteria tray back to the table, he tripped over an outstretched leg. Down he went, launching the tray into space. Mashed potatoes spattered over the heads of nearby students, and chocolate milk spilled all over Mrs. Montgomery's yellow dress. Julien was <u>mortified</u>. He jumped up, wiped the ketchup from his eyes, and dashed out of the lunchroom.

> *Context clues:* The context clues help you imagine how Julien must have felt. From the description of events and Julien's reaction to them, you can infer that *mortified* means "greatly embarrassed" or "humiliated."

Exercises

On a separate sheet of paper, explain how your knowledge and experience can help you infer the meaning of each underlined word.

1. Joey moaned and groaned, complaining about his head aching and his stomach churning. Mom listened patiently, knowing full well that Joey was only <u>feigning</u> illness to escape his math test. Then she calmly told him to get up, get dressed, and get to school.

2. "I need to find someone <u>adept</u> at fixing computers," Mr. Daniels cried, springing up from the chair. "I don't understand what these blasted error messages mean. What I *do* understand is that this high-tech gizmo just isn't working!"

3. The two neighbors glared at each other in silence. Though their houses were scarcely thirty feet apart, and their children were friends, the two women refused to exchange a word of greeting. When this <u>enmity</u> had begun or what had caused it was a mystery, but over the years it had only grown more intense.

WRITING SKILL BUILDER

Stating and Supporting a Position

Some writing assignments require you to take a clear position on an issue. That is, you have to state your viewpoint or opinion and then support it convincingly. Your supporting information may include specific reasons, facts, details, or examples.

For short assignments, such as a response to an essay question on a test, you will usually find it helpful to state your position in a *topic sentence*. A topic sentence focuses your writing and leads the reader directly into the information that follows. For longer assignments, such as an essay or report, you will similarly find it useful to state your position in a *thesis statement* (see Lesson 2, page 21 and Lesson 3, page 31).

After establishing your position in a topic sentence or thesis statement, develop your ideas with specific supporting details. It is not enough simply to express your point of view. You have to support your viewpoint with solid, persuasive information.

Activity

Some people believe that putting health warnings on cigarette packages is not enough. They feel that the government must do more to protect the public. In fact, cigarettes should be made illegal, and smoking should be banned. Do you agree or disagree with this idea? Why?

On a separate sheet of paper, write a response of two or more paragraphs expressing your views about this issue. Be specific, and support your position with clear reasons, facts, details, or examples. Try to persuade your reader. In your response, use at least two of the words that you have learned in this lesson.

LESSON 2

Some of the words that you will encounter on pages 12–14 and
15–16 of this lesson appear in bold type in the following paragraph.
Read the paragraph, and on a separate sheet of paper, answer the
questions that follow.

> Though Ezra had never had much interest in computers as a
> child, programming them became his **forte** as a teenager.
> Whereas at age 11 he had **idolized** ball players and rock stars,
> by age 15 it was technological wizards whom he admired most.
> The software problems that **demoralized** other people only
> encouraged Ezra to work harder. When it came to interacting
> with people, he was perhaps not the master of **diplomacy**, but
> sitting in front of a monitor, Ezra was unquestionably the king.

What is the main idea of this paragraph? Would you want Ezra as
your friend? Why or why not?

 LESSON WORDS 1–10: Pronounce the word, spell it, study
its meanings, and finish the sentence that follows it.

---

abyss (*n.*)   immeasurably deep or great space; bottomless depth;
ə-'bis   **chasm; gulf; void**

   1. From the edge of the (forest, cliff) _____, we looked
     down into the *abyss*.

acumen (*n.*)   keenness of perception or judgment; **discernment;**
ə-'kyü-mən   **insight; discrimination**

   2. The owner's business *acumen* helped the company (suc-
     ceed, fail) _____.

anecdote (*n.*)   short account of an interesting, amusing, or
'a-nik-ˌdōt   biographical incident or event, often intended to
entertain or illustrate; **story**; **tale**; **episode**

3. An experienced (speaker, physician) _____ is
always prepared with an *anecdote*.

castigate (*v.*)   subject to severe criticism or punishment; **rebuke**;
'kas-te-ˌgāt   **reprimand**

4. The magazine article *castigated* the corporation for its
(corruption, innovation) _____.

circuitous (*adj.*)   having a circular or winding course;
ˌsər-'kyü-ə-təs   **roundabout**; **indirect**

5. Jill would have arrived (later, sooner) _____ if she
had taken a less *circuitous* route.

compulsory (*adj.*)   required or compelled; **mandatory**;
kəm-'pəl-sə-rē   **obligatory**

6. The conference room was nearly (empty, full)
_____ because attendance at the meeting was *compulsory*.

demoralize (*v.*)   lower the morale of; **discourage**; **dishearten**
di-'mȯr-ə-ˌlīz

7. If you hope to become successful, you cannot let one (setback, triumph) _____ *demoralize* you.

denigrate (*v.*)   to attack the reputation or character of; **defame**;
'de-ni-ˌgrāt   **disparage**; **slander**

8. We were determined to (defend, attack) _____ the
candidate after the editorial had *denigrated* her.

diplomacy (*n.*)   skill in dealing with people or handling affairs; **tact**;
də-'plō-mə-sē   **discretion**

9. *Diplomacy* plays an essential role in (sculpture, politics)
_____.

exculpate (*v.*)   clear from alleged fault, blame, or guilt; **exonerate**;
'ek-,skəl-,pāt   **absolve**

10. The judge (imprisoned, freed) _____ the man
when it became clear that the evidence would *exculpate*
him.

B   **SENTENCE COMPLETION 1–10:** Enter the required lesson words.

---

1. The malicious rumors had _____**d** Mr. Patton, but he
remained confident that the ongoing investigation would
_____ him.

2. In the novel, scientists drill to the center of the planet, hoping to
descend into the _____, but they are _____**d**
when their plan fails.

3. Ruben is a master of _____, who can handle even
the most awkward social situations by telling a humorous
_____.

4. At some companies, retirement becomes _____
at a certain age, and employees must use their financial
_____ to budget their savings wisely for the years
ahead.

5. The supervisor _____**d** the travel agent for giving
_____ driving directions.

C   **VOCABULARY IN CONTEXT 1–10:** Read the paragraph,
and on a separate sheet of paper, answer the questions
that follow. Do not repeat any of the underlined words in
your answers; use synonyms instead.

Mr. Ford, the renowned mountain climber, began his speech
with a fascinating underline{anecdote} about his recent experience in the
Himalayas. He described the underline{circuitous} route he and his fellow
climbers had to take when an avalanche blocked their path.
Several times they all nearly plunged into the underline{abyss}, but they

refused to let the challenges they faced <u>demoralize</u> them. Although Ford has some critics who <u>denigrate</u> him, his audience that night had nothing but admiration for the man.

1. Paraphrase the paragraph.

2. Would you start an essay with an anecdote? Explain your answer.

 LESSON WORDS 11–20: Pronounce the word, spell it, study its meanings, and finish the sentence that follows it.

---

forte (*n.*)   person's strong point; **strength**; **specialty**
'fȯrt

> 11. Swimming is Jennifer's *forte* because she (loves, fears) _____ the water.

gratuitous (*adj.*)   not called for by the circumstances; **unjustified**;
grə-'tü-ə-təs   **unwarranted**; **unnecessary**

> 12. The villain in this movie shoots everyone in sight, which is too (little, much) _____ *gratuitous* violence for most viewers.

idolize (*v.*)   love or admire greatly or excessively; **worship**; **adore**
'ī-dᵊl-ˌīz

> 13. Jessica *idolized* her older brother; in her eyes he could do nothing (right, wrong) _____.

impart (*v.*)   to communicate the knowledge of; **disclose**; **reveal**;
im-'pärt   **convey**

> 14. The conspirators *imparted* their plans to (everyone, no one) _____.

inimical (*adj.*)   adverse, unfavorable, or hostile; **antagonistic**;
i-'ni-mi-kəl   **opposed**

> 15. Her mother's *inimical* expression told Sarah that this was a (wise, foolish) _____ time to ask to borrow the car.

interim (*n.*)   intervening time; **meantime**; **interval**
'in-tə-rəm

> 16. The new club president takes over (today, next month)
> _____; Eileen will hold the office in the *interim*.

intermittent (*adj.*)   starting and stopping intervals; **periodic**;
,in-tər-'mi-,t°nt   **discontinuous**

> 17. *Intermittent* thunderstorms (repeatedly, never)
> _____ disrupted our picnic.

pensive (*adj.*)   marked by or engaged in deep, serious, or sad
'pen(t)-siv   thought; **meditative**; **contemplative**

> 18. Dad sat in the chair, (quietly, noisily) _____
> *pensive*.

tome (*n.*)   book, especially a large, heavy, or scholarly book;
'tōm   **volume**; **work**

> 19. Bryan planned to read the *tome* over the next three (hours,
> weeks) _____.

tryst (*n.*)   appointment to meet at a certain time and place,
'trist   especially one made secretly by lovers; **assignation**;
        rendezvous

> 20. Roland and Julia found the most (private, public)
> _____ place they could for their *tryst*.

E **SENTENCE COMPLETION 11–20:** Enter the required
lesson words from D, above.

---

1. Despite the forecast of _____ showers, Michael and
Sonia planned their romantic _____ for four o'clock in
the park.

2. Clayton sat at the corner table in the library, a(n) _____
expression on his face, as he turned the pages of the dusty old
_____ before him.

3. Dad's _____ frown told me that he strongly disap-
proved of the video game's _____ carnage.

4. In the _____ before she took office, Marla's predeces-
sor _____**ed** to her several significant pieces of advice.

5. Even though baseball is not Richard's _____, he still
_____**s** the New York Yankees.

F **VOCABULARY IN CONTEXT 11–20**: Read the paragraph,
and on a separate sheet of paper, answer the questions
that follow. Do not repeat any of the underlined words in
your answers; use synonyms instead.

What can be more boring than having the flu? You're trapped
in the house, feeling alternately hot and cold because of your
intermittent fever. There's nothing to do except watch TV or
turn the pages of some old tome that's been sitting on your
shelf since the beginning of time. In the interim before you can
return to school, you stare out the window, a pensive expression on your face, wondering what wisdom your teachers may
be imparting to the class.

1. List the main idea and two supporting ideas for this paragraph.

2. Do you share the writer's feelings? Why or why not?

G **SYNONYMS**: To avoid repetition, replace the boldfaced
word with a synonym from the vocabulary list below.

---

mandatory	worship	roundabout	periodic	unwarranted
contemplative	discourage	exonerate	interval	tact

1. Even though the electrician's wiring is
rather **circuitous**, the completed
circuits operate as required.   1. _____

2. The interim government appointed
several well-respected individuals to
serve for the three-month **interim**.   2. _____

3. Because school attendance is **compulsory**, the state can compel students to come to class.

3. _____

4. Superhero statues were arranged like idols on the boy's shelf; it was clear that he **idolized** them.

4. _____**ed**

5. The waiter's **gratuitous** rudeness guaranteed that we would not leave him much of a gratuity.

5. _____

6. The moral of the story is that you should not let minor obstacles **demoralize** you.

6. _____

7. During the show's intermission, we stepped outside to see if the afternoon's **intermittent** snowfall had left any accumulation on the streets.

7. _____

8. As a newly appointed diplomat, O'Hara still had much to learn about handling foreign representatives with **diplomacy**.

8. _____

9. The poet stared pensively into space, her brow wrinkled in **pensive** concentration.

9. _____

10. Exculpating himself from the charge of plagiarism took considerable effort; his friends worried that he would not be **exculpated**.

10. _____**d**

H **ANTONYMS:** In the blank space in each sentence below, enter the word most nearly the antonym of the boldfaced word. Choose your antonyms from the following list.

direct	positive	optional	praise	steady
weakness	encourage	commend	abhor	necessary

1. Constructive criticism is a(n) _____ part of the revision process, but purely negative comments would be **gratuitous**.

2. Mr. Gomez was surprised by his supervisor's **inimical** reaction to the proposal because he had expected a more _____ response.

3. We took a **circuitous** route to the beach but returned along a much more _____ highway.

4. Fans can be fickle in their loyalties: the performer they **idolize** today, they may _____ tomorrow.

5. While some members of the audience **castigated** the speaker for her words, others _____**ed** her.

6. After falling behind in the first period, team members were **demoralized**, but the coach did her best to _____ them.

7. My **forte** is writing, although I must admit that spelling remains a(n) _____ of mine.

8. The warning feature on this electronic device begins with an **intermittent** beeping, which then changes to a(n) _____ whine after two minutes.

9. Members of the debating team were all good sports; they _____**d** their opponents rather than **denigrate** them.

10. Joining monthly discussion groups is _____ at our club, but participating in community service activities is **compulsory**.

CONCISE WRITING: Express the thought of each sentence in NO MORE THAN FOUR WORDS.

---

1. The short account of an interesting incident that Dave presented caused us to be amused.

_____

2. Being defeated resulted in the morale of the members of our team becoming lower.

_____

3. The appointment we had made to meet secretly at a particular time and place was put off until a later time.

_____

4. Leyla stayed as she was, not saying a word, looking very thoughtful and a little sad.

_____

5. What you are assuming is by no means called for by the circumstances.

_____

6. To be successful in politics, one must have skill in dealing with people.

_____

 VOCABULARY SKILL BUILDER

Etymologies

The _etymology_ of a word is its history and origin. You can expand your knowledge of language by reading the etymologies of words that you look up in the dictionary. In addition, you will find that many etymologies are genuinely interesting. For example, did you know that the word _dandelion_ comes from _dent de lion_, meaning "tooth of the lion"? This meaning is derived from the dandelion flower's tooth-shaped leaves.

Exercises

Each of the following words appears as a lesson word or a synonym in Lesson 1 or 2. Look up the etymology of each word. On a separate sheet of paper, briefly summarize the word's history and derivation.

1. abyss	4. forte	7. interval	10. shy
2. denigrate	5. impromptu	8. rendezvous	11. squalid
3. enmity	6. inimical	9. rouse	12. timid

WRITING SKILL BUILDER

Writing Effective Essays

An *essay* is a composition of several paragraphs that deals with a particular topic from the writer's viewpoint. An essay should have a clear central idea, which is usually introduced in a *thesis statement.* A well-written thesis statement is clear and specific, not vague or overly broad.

A strong thesis statement helps to focus your writing. Compare the following examples:

> *Too broad:* Driving requires practice.

> *More specific:* To become a safe driver, a teenager must first learn the rules of the road and then practice driving under various road conditions.

Every paragraph in an essay should relate to the central idea. Just as the supporting information in a paragraph develops the topic sentence, so should the supporting paragraphs in an essay develop the central idea.

Activity

Complete the following statement: *The single most important quality for a friend to have is* _____. Be sure that you have specific reasons in mind to support your opinion.

On a separate sheet of paper, write an essay expressing your point of view about "the most important quality for a friend to have." Your essay should have a clear central idea, and every paragraph should relate to this idea. State your central idea in a thesis statement, and support your position with specific reasons, facts, details, or examples. In your essay, use at least two of the words that you have learned in this lesson.

LESSON 3

Lesson Preview

Some of the words that you will encounter on pages 22–24 and 25–26 of this lesson appear in bold type in the following poem. Read the poem, and on a separate sheet of paper, answer the questions that follow.

> The **taciturn** old traveler
> Had not a single word to say.
> He carried a beat-up **valise**,
> And slowly he went on his way.
>
> Parents **admonished** their kids:
> "A **disreputable** tramp is he."
> But just a harmless, lonely man—
> This was all that I could see.

What is this poem about? How do the poet's feelings differ from the feelings of the parents mentioned in the second stanza?

 LESSON WORDS 1–10: Pronounce the word, spell it, study its meanings, and finish the sentence that follows it.

---

admonish (*v.*)   express warning or disapproval to, especially in a
ad-'mä-nish   gentle, sincere way; **reprove**; **scold**; **reprimand**

   1. The teacher *admonished* the student for coming to class
     (promptly, late) _____ .

artifice (*n.*)   clever or ingenious device; **trick**; **ruse**; **ploy**
'är-tə-fəs

   2. Secret agents must use every *artifice* they can in order to
     (escape, entertain) _____ their enemies.

bellicose (*adj.*)   favoring or inclined to fight or quarrel; **warlike**;
'be-li-ˌkōs   **quarrelsome**; **belligerent**

> 3. The dictator's *bellicose* attitude made him (popular, unpopu-
> lar) _____ with neighboring countries.

characterize (*v.*)   be a characteristic or feature of; **distinguish**;
'kar-ik-tə-ˌrīz   **define**; **typify**

> 4. Many (poems, paintings) _____ are *characterized*
> by imaginative similes and metaphors.

coy (*adj.*)   pretending to be shy; **bashful**; **modest**; **reserved**
'kȯi

> 5. Anna's (quiet, loud) _____ response was typical of
> her *coy* manner.

disreputable (*adj.*)   having a bad reputation; not reputable or
dis-'re-pyə-tə-bəl   respectable; **notorious**; **disgraceful**;
                discreditable

> 6. A *disreputable* car salesman is (worthy, unworthy)
> _____ of your trust.

dissension (*n.*)   difference of opinion; **disagreement**; **discord**;
di-'sen-shən   **quarreling**

> 7. Political *dissension* threatened to (split, unite)
> _____ the government.

espouse (*v.*)   take up and support as a cause; **adopt**; **advocate**;
is-'paůz   **embrace**

> 8. As a proponent of (democracy, dictatorship) _____,
> the writer *espouses* equal rights for all.

foray (*n.*)   sudden invasion or attack for war or plunder; **raid**;
'fȯr-ˌā   **incursion**

> 9. Rebels made *forays* into the villages, (contributing, stealing)
> _____ whatever they could.

frenetic (*adj.*)   marked by frenzy; **frantic**; **hectic**; **frenzied**
fri-'ne-tik

10. The *frenetic* pace of a commuter's life leaves (much, little) _____ time for relaxation.

B   **SENTENCE COMPLETION 1–10:** Enter the required lesson words.

---

1. The young woman's _____ behavior was nothing more than a(n) _____ she used to attract suitors.

2. The _____ company sold poor-quality merchandize _____**d** by loose parts and chipped paint.

3. There was widespread _____ in the council, as _____ members tried to persuade more passive citizens that it was time to attack.

4. Although the captain _____**d** peace, he was prepared to order a(n) _____ into the neighboring town.

5. Dad _____**ed** my sister for keeping up such a(n) _____ pace all weekend that she was exhausted by Sunday night.

C   **VOCABULARY IN CONTEXT 1–10:** Read the paragraph, and on a separate sheet of paper, answer the questions that follow. Do not repeat any of the underlined words in your answers; use synonyms instead.

The duke of Westfield was a disreputable individual, known for his short temper and bellicose nature. Nevertheless, preparations for his wedding continued at a frenetic pace, and dissension within the royal court was set aside. After all, the duke was the queen's first-born son. His marriage celebration would be characterized by all the extravagant display one would expect.

1. Paraphrase the paragraph.

2. Explain the meaning of the last sentence.

D | **LESSON WORDS 11–20:** Pronounce the word, spell it, study its meanings, and finish the sentence that follows it.

impasse (*n.*)   situation offering no obvious escape; **deadlock**;
'im-,pas   **standoff**

11. When jurors came to an *impasse* in their deliberations, they were (able, unable) _____ to reach a verdict.

implicate (*v.*)   show to be connected or involved; **associate**;
'im–plə-,kāt   **incriminate; involve**

12. The (insufficient, abundant) _____ evidence that *implicated* Mr. Jackson in the crime led to his conviction.

pervasive (*adj.*)   tending to pervade or spread throughout;
per-'vā-siv   **enveloping; all-encompassing**

13. Entering the forest, the hikers immediately noticed the *pervasive* (scent, height) _____ of pine trees.

petulant (*adj.*)   tending to be easily or unpredictably ill-humored;
'pe-chə-lənt   **peevish; irritable**

14. Children sometimes become *petulant* when they are (tired, enthusiastic) _____ .

quizzical (*adj.*)   expressing puzzlement, curiosity, or disbelief;
'kwi-zi-kəl   **questioning; perplexed**

15. The *quizzical* expression on her face told me that she had (managed, failed) _____ to solve the riddle.

scrutinize (*v.*)   examine closely and carefully; **inspect; study**
'skrü-t³n-,īz

16. Detectives spent nearly five (minutes, hours) _____ *scrutinizing* the crime scene.

specious (*adj.*)   having a false appearance of truth, logic, or
'spē-shəs   genuineness; **erroneous**; **fallacious**

17. Once the jury realized that the defense lawyer's argument
    was *specious*, they concluded that the defendant was (inno-
    cent, guilty) _____ .

taciturn (*adj.*)   not inclined to speak; **uncommunicative**;
'ta-sə-,tərn   **reticent**; **silent**

18. Because Les is such a *taciturn* young man, it is (easy,
    difficult) _____ to know what he is thinking.

ultimatum (*n.*)   final offer or demand, especially one whose
,əl-tə-'mā-təm   rejection will end negotiations and result in the
                use of force, a break in relations, or punitive
                action; **demand**; **requirement**

19. When a country ignores a neighboring country's *ultimatum*,
    the result is likely to be (peace, war) _____ .

valise (*n.*)   portable case for holding a traveler's clothes and
və-lēs   personal articles; **suitcase**; **satchel**

20. The airline temporarily misplaced my *valise*, so I had noth-
    ing to (wear, do) _____ .

E   **SENTENCE COMPLETION 11–20:** Enter the required
     lesson words from D, above.

---

1. Treaty negotiations had reached a(n) _____, and each
   side presented the other with a(n) _____ .

2. The investigator had a(n) _____ look on her face as she
   _____d what some believed to be a forged document.

3. Although witnesses _____d the man in the theft of the
   _____, he denied having been anywhere near the air-
   port baggage area.

4. "Your reasoning is _____," the professor said, but the
   _____ young woman made no reply.

5. In the story, the troll is a(n) _____ and unpleasant crea-
ture, whose _____ ill humor cast everything in a negative light.

VOCABULARY IN CONTEXT 11–20: Read the paragraph, and on a separate sheet of paper, answer the questions that follow. Do not repeat any of the underlined words in your answers; use synonyms instead.

Attorneys from both sides scrutinized the proposed compromise. If they could not get past their impasse, employees would
go on strike at midnight. The pervasive tension in the conference room had everyone fidgeting in their seats. Finally, one of
the more taciturn lawyers looked up, a quizzical expression on
his face. "Where did you ever get the idea that we would agree
to such a large salary increase?" he asked, in a petulant tone.

1. What is this paragraph about?

2. Do you think the two sides are close to settlement? Why or why
not?

G

SYNONYMS: To avoid repetition, replace the boldfaced word with a synonym from the vocabulary list below.

---

deadlock	study	define	involve	discord
notorious	hectic	peevish	advocate	reticent

1. "From now on, I will take my business
to a reputable store," shouted Mulligan,
"not to a **disreputable** swindler like
you!"   1. _____

2. Martha is a strong believer in capitalism,
but her spouse **espouses** a socialist
point of view.   2. _____s

3. If a compromise settlement does not
allow us to move past this **impasse**,
our meeting may go on all night.   3. _____

4. When Gregory behaved like a **petulant** child, his friends soon lost patience with his petulance.   4. _____

5. Shriya, the most **taciturn** member of the city council, gave tacit approval to the proposed plan.   5. _____

6. Generosity is the feature that best **characterizes** Mrs. Steger's character.   6. _____**s**

7. The news article **implicated** Mr. Williamson, though he strongly denied any implication of improper behavior.   7. _____**d**

8. The government had the suspected spy under 24-hour scrutiny, and agents **scrutinized** his every move.   8. _____**ed**

9. Political dissent is part of the democratic process, but at times the **dissension** can get out of hand.   9. _____

10. The candidates were in a frenzy during the **frenetic** final days of the campaign.   10. _____

H **ANTONYMS:** In the blank space in each sentence below, enter the word most nearly the antonym of the boldfaced word. Choose your antonyms from the following list.

---

valid	commend	calm	talkative	easygoing
limited	agreement	respectable	clear	good-natured

1. Over time, **disreputable** stores lose their customers to more _____ establishments.

2. The photograph that had at first **implicated** the bank teller in the robbery eventually helped to _____ him.

3. The novel's main character is a(n) _____ construction worker named Scott, who is negatively influenced by his more **bellicose** brother.

4. The bloody violence that was once _____ to a few scenes in a horror film is now **pervasive** in many movies.

5. General _____ among the members of Congress regarding this bill was a welcome change from the usual **dissension**.

6. The two mathematicians debated for an hour, one of them insisting that her analysis was perfectly _____, while the other argued that the underlying logic was **specious**.

7. After a **frenetic** day on Wall Street, the stock broker was relieved to return to her _____ suburban home.

8. The head of our department, a man who is normally very _____, becomes **petulant** when he is under stress.

9. The counselors _____ed the campers for some of their actions, but **admonished** them for some of the other things that they had done.

10. Marielle had been shy and **taciturn** as a young girl, but she became much more _____ when she entered her teens.

CONCISE WRITING: Express the thought of each sentence in NO MORE THAN FOUR WORDS.

---

1. The patriot took up freedom as a cause and supported it.

_____

2. The people who were negotiating came to a situation that offered no obvious way out.

_____

3. The expression on Emma's face expressed puzzlement, curiosity, or disbelief.

_____

4. Every night, soldiers carried out sudden attacks.

_____

5. The administrative head of the school expressed disapproval to Brendan in a gentle, sincere way.

_____

6. The point you are arguing has a false appearance of logic.

_____

 VOCABULARY SKILL BUILDER

Word Parts: Prefixes and Suffixes

Many words are made up of parts. For example, the word _inspection_ is a combination of three parts:

_in-_	+	_spec_	+	_-tion_
prefix		root		suffix

Spec is a _root_, a word part from which other words are formed. _In-_ is a prefix, while _-tion_ is a suffix. _Prefixes_ and _suffixes_ are groups of letters added to the beginning (prefix) or end (suffix) of a word or root, changing its meaning or forming a new word. A word may have one or more prefixes and suffixes.

Your knowledge of word parts can help you figure out the meaning of unfamiliar words and enlarge your vocabulary.

Some of the vocabulary words in this lesson and in previous lessons use the common prefixes and suffixes shown below:

Prefix	Meaning	Example
dis-	"not" or "the opposite of"	discourage
in-, im-	"in" or "into"	insight
un-	"not" or "the opposite of"	unjustified

Suffix	Meaning	Example
-able	"capable of being," "worthy of being"	detestable
-ive	"inclined to," "tending to"	pervasive
-ment	"condition of being"; also, "action," "process," or "result"	requirement
-ion, -tion, -sion	"action," "state," or "condition"	incursion

Exercises

Each of the following words appears as a lesson word or a synonym in this lesson or in a previous lesson. Circle the prefix and/or suffix in each word. Then, on a separate sheet of paper, write a sentence using the word. You may use more than one word in the same sentence. If you need help, check a dictionary.

1. disreputable
2. uncommunicative
3. discretion
4. inspect

5. dissension
6. offensive
7. disagreement
8. discreditable

WRITING SKILL BUILDER

Essay Structure

You've learned that an essay should have a clear central idea—usually expressed in a thesis statement—and every paragraph should relate to this idea. Essays generally have three parts: an introduction, a body, and a conclusion. The introduction introduces the essay topic and states the central idea. The body supports and develops this idea. The conclusion brings the essay to a close.

Activity

Some educators think that schools do not spend enough time teaching and discussing current events. As a result, students are not as informed about the world as they should be. What's your opinion? How important is it for young people to understand what is going on in the world? Should schools do more to help students become well-informed citizens?

Express your views in an essay. Include an introduction, body, and conclusion. Be sure that your essay has a clear central idea and that every paragraph relates to this idea. Remember that it is not enough simply to express your opinion. You have to support your point of view with solid, persuasive information: specific reasons, facts, details, or examples. In your essay, use at least two of the words that you have learned in this lesson. Write your essay on a separate sheet of paper.

LESSON 4

Some of the words that you will encounter on pages 33–35 and 36–37 of this lesson appear in bold type in the following paragraph. Read the paragraph, and on a separate sheet of paper, answer the questions that follow.

> It is **inevitable** that Robert will someday make a career of writing. After all, ever since he was old enough to print his name, Robert has **aspired** to be a writer. While everyone occasionally exaggerates when they speak, Robert **embellishes** every story he tells. In fact, he is such a **loquacious** and imaginative young man that most people are relieved when Robert finally stops talking and starts writing.

What is this paragraph about? How does context—the surrounding words and sentences—help you infer the meaning of the boldfaced words?

 LESSON WORDS 1–10: Pronounce the word, spell it, study its meanings, and finish the sentence that follows it.

---

aspire (*v.*)   seek to attain or accomplish a certain goal; **seek**; **aim**
ə-'spīr

  1. If you *aspire* to become wealthy, you will have to find a (pleasant, lucrative) _____ job.

despicable (*adj.*)   deserving to be despised; **contemptible**; **vile**
di-'spi-kə-bəl

  2. "Such thoroughly *despicable* behavior," said the judge, "deserves the (maximum, minimum) _____ sentence."

destitute (*adj.*)   lacking the necessities of life; living in extreme
'des-tə-,tüt   poverty; **impoverished; penniless**

>   3. The farmers were left *destitute* by the (drought, eclipse)
>   _____ .

embellish (*v.*)   make more interesting or attractive by adding
im-'be-lish   details, often of a fictitious or imaginary nature;
        embroider; enhance

>   4. Trudy hoped to (strengthen, impress) _____ the
>   interviewer by *embellishing* her work experience.

enrage (*v.*)   make very angry; **infuriate; incense**
in-'rāj

>   5. Mr. Karp was *enraged* when his neighbor (admired, dented)
>   _____ his new car.

fastidious (*adj.*)   demanding excessive care or delicacy; difficult to
fa-'sti-dē-əs   please; **exacting; fussy**

>   6. Juan is so *fastidious* about his appearance that he spends
>   ten (minutes, seconds) _____ combing his hair.

gloat (*v.*)   observe or think about with triumphant and often
'glōt   malicious satisfaction or pleasure; **revel; rejoice**

>   7. The athlete *gloated* over his rival's (misfortune, good for-
>   tune) _____ .

hierarchy (*n.*)   organization of a group of people or things, one
'hī-ər-,är-kē   above the other, according to rank, class, or grade;
        ladder; chain of command

>   8. The company president held the (highest, lowest)
>   _____ position in the corporate *hierarchy*.

inevitable (*adj.*)   cannot be avoided or evaded; certain to occur;
i-'ne-və-tə-bəl   **unavoidable; inescapable**

>   9. Having taken such (good, poor) _____ care of his
>   old car, Felipe knew that a breakdown was *inevitable*.

ingenuous (*adj.*)   showing innocent or childlike simplicity and
in-′jen-yə-wəs   candidness; **sincere**; **frank**; **guileless**

> 10. Her *ingenuous* smile made clear that any offense given by
> the remark was (deliberate, unintentional) _____.

SENTENCE COMPLETION 1–10: Enter the required lesson
words.

---

1. The town's citizens were _____**ed** when they learned
   of the man's _____ crimes.

2. As Danford advanced within the _____ of government,
   she never _____**ed** over her rivals' setbacks.

3. Because Tim had always been such a(n) _____ dresser,
   no one was surprised that he _____**d** to a career in
   fashion design.

4. Gina's _____ response suggested that she had no idea
   just how much Ron had _____**ed** his account of
   events.

5. Once the region's only factory went out of business, it
   was _____ that some workers would be left

   _____ .

VOCABULARY IN CONTEXT 1–10: Read the paragraph,
and on a separate sheet of paper, answer the questions
that follow. Do not repeat any of the underlined words in
your answers; use synonyms instead.

Last night we watched a silly old western about a <u>despicable</u>
villain who swindles a widow out of her property, leaving the
woman homeless and <u>destitute</u>. When the townspeople find out
what the villain has done, they are <u>enraged</u>. The ending, of
course, is <u>inevitable</u>. The villain goes to prison, and the kindly
old lady gets her home back.

1. Rewrite the paragraph with the same story but set in a city in the present.

2. Suppose you were a scriptwriter asked to improve this plot. How might you embellish the story?

D | **LESSON WORDS 11–20:** Pronounce the word, spell it, study its meanings, and finish the sentence that follows it.

---

intricacy (*n.*)   quality or state of being intricate; **complexity**;
'in-tri-kə-sē   **elaborateness**

11. The *intricacy* of the jigsaw puzzle made it (easy, challenging) _____ to solve

loquacious (*adj.*)   given to excessive talking; **talkative**;
lō-kwā-shəs   **garrulous**

12. No one is more *loquacious* than Aunt Dorothy, who (seldom, always) _____ has a story to tell.

opulent (*adj.*)   showing wealth or affluence; very rich; **lavish**;
'ä-pyə-lənt   **luxurious**

13. After ten (prosperous, unsuccessful) _____ years, the architect relocated to an *opulent* office downtown.

poignant (*adj.*)   deeply affecting the feelings, especially evoking
'poi-nyənt   pity, compassion, or sadness; **touching**; **moving**

14. The book reviewer described the novel as "a *poignant* story of two children and their beloved dog, sure to elicit (laughter, tears) _____ from young and old alike."

precipice (*n.*)   very steep or overhanging rock face; **cliff**; **crag**
'pre-sə-pəs

15. A high fence around the (summit, bottom) _____ of the mountain kept hikers from slipping over the *precipice*.

pretentious (*adj.*)   making or implying usually unjustified or
pri-'ten(t)-shəs   exaggerated claims to some distinction or
importance; **affected**; **ostentatious**

16. It was *pretentious* of the (parking attendant, car mechanic)
_____ to refer to himself as a "auto specialist."

proponent (*n.*)   person who argues in favor of something, such as
prə-'pō-nənt   a cause; **advocate**; **supporter**

17. As a strong *proponent* of women's sports, the teacher (pro-
moted, opposed) _____ the creation of a girls' fenc-
ing team.

subterfuge (*n.*)   plan, action, or device used to conceal, escape, or
'səb-tər-,fyüj   evade; **ploy**; **ruse**; **artifice**

18. Only a businessman who is (unscrupulous, trustworthy)
_____ would obtain the deed to a property by *subterfuge*.

surmise (*v.*)   form a notion from very little evidence; **infer**;
sər-'mīz   **conclude**; **guess**

19. Based on a (fingerprint, confession) _____,
Inspector Dillingsworth *surmised* that someone on the
museum staff had stolen the painting.

torrid (*adj.*)   intensely hot; **scorching**; **burning**
'tȯr-əd *or*
'tär-əd

20. The travelers knew that without (water, blankets)
_____ they could not survive their journey across
the *torrid* desert.

SENTENCE COMPLETION 11–20: Enter the required lesson words from D, above.

1. Though some people regarded the actor's newly constructed mansion as a(n) _____ masterpiece, others viewed the enormous structure as a(n) _____ eyesore.

2. The climbers advanced slowly along the _____, the _____ weather hindering their progress.

3. Since Karen would never have sold the rare coins had she known their true value, we can only _____ that the buyer acquired them by _____.

4. The book was a(n) _____ tale of a family's struggle to remain together, but the _____ of the plot made it difficult to follow the narrative flow.

5. The governor, who is usually quite _____, did not have much to say about the proposed law because he is not one of its strongest _____s.

VOCABULARY IN CONTEXT 11–20: Read the paragraph, and on a separate sheet of paper, answer the questions that follow. Do not repeat any of the underlined words in your answers; use synonyms instead.

Pedro La Vaca is without doubt the most <u>pretentious</u> artist in all of Spain. He brags incessantly about the <u>intricacy</u> of his oil paintings, although even a child could paint as well as this <u>loquacious</u> bore. As a highly regarded artist myself, as well as a leading <u>proponent</u> of artistic experimentation, I take offense at La Vaca's claims to talent. I can only <u>surmise</u> that the man has inhaled so many paint fumes that he now manages to delude himself into believing that bright colors randomly splashed onto a canvas magically create worthwhile artwork.

1. Paraphrase the paragraph.

2. How would you describe the tone of this paragraph?

3. What kind of a person do you think the writer is? Explain your answer.

 SYNONYMS: To avoid repetition, replace the boldfaced word with a synonym from the vocabulary list below.

---

luxurious	cliff	vile	enhance	seek
supporter	affected	infuriate	inescapable	complexity

1. Bethany became **enraged** when her brother took her cell phone, and her rage increased when he refused to give it back.

    1. _____**d**

2. The **intricacy** of this case stumped even Sherlock Holmes, who had solved so many intricate crimes in the past.

    2. _____

3. Kyle **aspires** to become a teacher, which is a laudable aspiration.

    3. _____**s**

4. The drive down the precipitous mountain road was terrifying; we feared we might go over a **precipice** at any moment.

    4. _____

5. The people despised the dictator for his **despicable** cruelty.

    5. _____

6. Certain events are **inevitable**; for example, night inevitably follows day.

    6. _____

7. The opulence of the new hotel was remarkable; never before had Andrew seen such **opulent** accommodations.

    7. _____

8. "Perhaps my expertise as a carpenter and a craftsman may be of some service, madam," the handyman said pretentiously. Meg tried not to smile at his **pretentious** manner of speaking.

    8. _____

9. The author **embellished** her account
   of Aztec civilization with a variety of
   imaginative embellishments.   9. _____ d

10. Senator Fodi is an enthusiastic
    proponent of the proposal to
    construct a new library.   10. _____

H   **ANTONYMS:** In the blank space in each sentence below,
         enter the word most nearly the antonym of the boldfaced
         word. Choose your antonyms from the following list.

---

calm	**avoidable**	**easygoing**	**simplicity**	**impoverished**
cold	**down-to-earth**	**taciturn**	**admirable**	**prosperous**

1. The **torrid** climate near the equator contrasts sharply with the
   _____ temperatures of the far north.

2. I am _____ about most activities but **fastidious** when
   it comes to my woodworking projects.

3. Technology has evolved from the _____ of early
   machines to the **intricacy** of modern computers.

4. Mrs. Saunders, who took over the store, is a(n) _____
   woman, so unlike the **despicable** previous owner.

5. It is surprising that Raymund is **loquacious** because his parents
   are both _____ people.

6. With our three best players injured, it is **inevitable** that we will
   lose this game, but we hope that a shutout will be

   _____.

7. As a result of the Great Depression, many once _____
   families found themselves **destitute**.

8. The _____ area on the east side of the Caribbean island
   stood in sharp contrast to the **opulent** tourist hotels on the west
   side.

9. The crowd was **enraged** at first, but police officers
   _____**ed** them.

10. Before she became a successful actress, Alexis was a(n)
_____ person; now she is as **pretentious** as most
other movie stars.

CONCISE WRITING: Express the thought of each sentence
in NO MORE THAN FOUR WORDS.

---

1. At times, children make the stories that they tell more interesting
by adding details that may not actually be true.

_____

2. The expression on Dara's face was one that reflected her innocent simplicity and candid nature.

_____

3. After you have achieved a victory, do not recall it with feelings of
malicious satisfaction.

_____

4. The surface of the rock that is projecting over us is covered with
ice.

_____

5. The plan that you devised in order to conceal the truth successfully deceived us.

_____

6. The poet's words deeply affect the reader's emotions, evoking
feelings of sadness.

_____

VOCABULARY SKILL BUILDER

Word Parts: Roots

Roots are combined with other word parts to form words. Here are some common roots:

Root	Meaning	Examples
spect, spec	"see," "look"	spectacle, aspect
ped	"foot"	pedestrian, centipede
voc, vok	"call"	vocation, invoke
mand	"order"	command, mandate

Exercises

1. Each of the following words appears as a vocabulary word in this lesson or in a previous lesson. Underline the root in each word. Then, on a separate sheet of paper, write a sentence using the word. You may use more than one word in the same sentence. If you need help, check a dictionary.

   a. provoke
   b. demand
   c. advocate
   d. inspect
   e. impede
   f. mandatory

2. How many other words can you identify that contain the root *ped* meaning "foot"?

WRITING SKILL BUILDER

Organizing Content: Order of Importance/Interest

When you write an essay, you develop ideas with supporting information. This information may include specific reasons, facts, details, or examples.

You can organize the content of a paragraph, or of an entire essay, in a various ways. For example, you can arrange your reasons, facts, details, and examples in order of *increasing* importance or interest,

progressing from the least important/interesting to the most impor-
tant/interesting. This approach is effective when you want to build to
a conclusion.

Or you can arrange your information in order of *decreasing*
importance or interest, moving from the most important/interesting
to the least important/interesting. This method works well when you
want to begin with a strong opening point and then follow with additional points.

Activity

Do you agree or disagree with the following statement? *Schools
place far too much emphasis on athletics.* Why?

On a separate sheet of paper, write an essay expressing your viewpoint on this question. Include an introduction, body, and conclusion. State your central idea in a thesis statement, and support your
position with solid, persuasive information. Organize your supporting
information in order of increasing or decreasing importance/interest.
In your essay, use at least two of the words that you have learned in
this lesson.

Unit I Review
and Enrichment

 CLOSE READING: Read the following statements. Then answer questions 1–10.

STATEMENTS

Jason was determined to become a dental surgeon, no matter how many more years of school that required.

"If you don't refund my money for this defective product," the customer said, "I'll never shop in this store again."

"I'll never win now," Andrew muttered, when his chess opponent captured his queen.

Jenny is an editorial assistant at a small publishing company; she reports to the associate editor, who in turn reports to the editor, who works directly for the company president.

By the time the professor had finally finished his lecture, half the class was dozing.

Liz thought that rock climbing was not challenging enough, so she took up hang gliding.

Brenda thought that Maya Angelou was not only a wonderful writer but also a fascinating person, and she wanted to be just like her.

After school, Corey and Marilyn met in a quiet part of the park to exchange valentines because they didn't want anyone to know that they were dating.

Having grown up rich and pampered, the young prince treated everyone as his inferior.

"Your hands are so dirty, Billy," Dad said. "Please scrub them before you come to the dinner table."

QUESTIONS

1. Who is loquacious? _____

2. Who was idolized? _____

3. Who has an imperious attitude? _____

4. Who had a tryst? _____

5. Who is part of a hierarchy? _____

6. Who has a penchant for taking risks? _____

7. Who delivered an ultimatum? _____

8. Who aspired to a particular career? _____

9. Who admonished someone? _____

10. Who was demoralized? _____

B **CONCISE WRITING:** Make the following passages more concise using no more than the number of words suggested.

---

1. A small number of people who are not respectable may act badly, but do not give in to the tendency to allow their actions to lower your morale. *(Cut to about 13 words.)*

---

2. The faces of the members of the audience expressed puzzlement, which enabled me to guess that my short account of an interesting incident was beyond the understanding of the people in the audience. *(Cut to about 18 words.)*

---

3. When she saw the filthy and wretched conditions under which the extremely poor families lived, Ms. Kellog, who was usually not inclined to say very much, became very, very angry and demanded that the government take some action to help. *(Cut to about 21 words.)*

_____

_____

4. The directions that you gave us for driving wound around all over the place, so there was absolutely no doubt that we would lose our way. *(Cut to about 14 words.)*

_____

5. The back-and-forth looks that the two men gave each other were filled with such feelings of hostility that it was quite clear the men viewed each other as enemies. *(Cut to about 13 words.)*

_____

 CLOSE READING: Read the following statements. Then answer questions 11–20.

STATEMENTS

"Even though I've only worked for the company a few months," said Kim, "I'm already one of the most skilled and valuable employees."

From John's vantage point, the people at the base of the mountain looked tiny.

Raul grabbed his bag and rushed to board the train.

The prime minister urged the assembly to launch an all-out attack on the rebel stronghold.

"We know that your identification papers are forged," said the police lieutenant.

Whenever Glen encountered a challenge, he doubted his ability to overcome it.

Melissa patiently showed her sister how to do use the computer to do research for school.

"I didn't break the lamp," cried Tony. "It was Alex."

Mr. Foxworth's home had 26 rooms, a swimming pool, and a tennis court.

No one ever questions Joanne's statements, because she would never lie.

QUESTIONS

11. Who is known for veracity? _____

12. Who had a diffident nature? _____

13. Who carried a valise? _____

14. Who imparted knowledge to someone else? _____

15. Who was pretentious? _____

16. Who was able to discern the truth? _____

17. Who implicated someone? _____

18. Who was bellicose? _____

19. Who had an opulent lifestyle? _____

20. Who was standing on a precipice? _____

D **ANALOGIES:** Which lettered pair of words—a, b, c, d, or e—most nearly has the same relationship as the numbered pair? Enter the letter of your answer in the space provided.

---

1. CLEAN : SQUALID
   a. fresh : sparkling   b. disreputable : infamous
   c. foul : unpleasant   d. calm : frenetic
   e. petulant : impatient   1. _____

2. ARTIFICE : DECEIVE

    a. innocence : feign   b. hint : help
    c. clue : examine   d. information : forget
    e. victory : gloat   2. _____

3. DEFEAT : DEMORALIZE

    a. subterfuge : encounter   b. dissension : assemble
    c. success : cooperate   d. philosophy : incite
    e. triumph : encourage   3. _____

4. LOQUACIOUS : TACITURN

    a. despondent : cheerful   b. garrulous : talkative
    c. enthusiastic : curious   d. circuitous : distant
    e. excessive : odious   4. _____

5. TOME : LIBRARY

    a. law : government   b. paint : house
    c. clothing : department store   d. window : building
    e. automobile : parking lot   5. _____

 VOCABULARY SKILL BUILDER

Do the following exercises on a separate sheet of paper.

1. Explain how your knowledge and experience can help you infer the meaning of each underlined word in the following paragraph.

    The side door of the theater opened, and Dusty Dander emerged, surrounded by three muscular bodyguards. Scores of young fans immediately began pushing forward, shouting his name. Clearly, they <u>idolized</u> the singer, despite what the media said about him. Newspapers and magazines had <u>implicated</u> Dusty in a wide range of <u>despicable</u> actions, from dealing drugs to accepting bribes. But none of that seemed to matter to the screaming crowd.

2. Look up each of the following words, and briefly summarize the word's etymology.

> bellicose   gloat   loquacious   subterfuge

3. Circle the prefix and/or suffix in each of the following words. Then use the word in a sentence.

> unavoidable   incursion   disreputable
> pervasive   disagreement   uncommunicative

LESSON 5

Some of the words that you will encounter on pages 50–52 and
53–54 of this lesson appear in bold type in the following poem. Read
the poem, and on a separate sheet of paper, answer the questions
that follow.

> The message Jack found was not **cryptic**—
> Its meaning was direct and clear.
> And the **grotesque** sketch that came with it
> Filled the young scientist with fear.
>
> "You've **plagiarized** my work," said the note,
> "Those are *my* ideas you've submitted.
> Such **brazen** and shocking thievery
> Simply will not be permitted!"

What is this poem about? What would you do if you were Jack?

 LESSON WORDS 1–10: Pronounce the word, spell it, study
its meanings, and finish the sentence that follows it.

---

accommodate (*v.*)   give consideration to; allow or provide for;
ə-'kä-mə-,dāt   **oblige**; **suit**; **reconcile**

1. In order to (inform, please) _____ voters, candidates for public office try to *accommodate* the interests of
many different groups.

acquisition (*n.*)   something or someone acquired, gained, or
,ə-kwə-'zi-shən   added; **addition**; **purchase**

2. The art museum's latest *acquisition* was made possible by
the (generosity, consistency) _____ of contributors.

50

ambivalent (*adj.*)   simultaneous, contradictory feelings toward an
am-'bi-və-lənt   object, person, idea, or action; **uncertain**;
                        conflicted

   3. I have (many, no) _____ doubts about whether
      your plan makes sense; my feelings are *ambivalent*.

benevolent (*adj.*)   marked by or disposed to doing good; **kindly**;
bə-'nə-və-lənt   **generous**; **altruistic**

   4. The queen's *benevolent* actions earned her many (friends,
      enemies) _____.

brazen (*adj.*)   showing contemptuous boldness; **shameless**;
'brā-zⁿn   **impudent**

   5. Parking a car next to a (curb, fire hydrant) _____
      shows a *brazen* disregard for the law.

cryptic (*adj.*)   having or appearing to have a hidden or ambiguous
'krip-tik   meaning; **mysterious**; **puzzling**

   6. An archaeologist well-known for breaking (records, codes)
      _____ was able to read the *cryptic* message
      inscribed on the ancient tablet.

enigmatic (*adj.*)   of or like an enigma; **ambiguous**; **mystifying**;
,e-nig-'ma-tik   **perplexing**

   7. The *enigmatic* play (delighted, puzzled) _____
      students in the literature class.

extricate (*v.*)   set free or remove from an entanglement or difficulty;
'ek-strə-,kāt   **release**; **disentangle**

   8. The company president hired a team of accountants to *extri-
      cate* the business from its financial (difficulties, achievements)
      _____.

fluctuate (*v.*)   change or vary continually or irregularly; **swing**;
'flək-chə-,wāt   **oscillate**

   9. Changing (road, weather) _____ conditions caused
      temperatures to *fluctuate* during the afternoon.

grimace (*n.*)   facial expression usually of pain, displeasure, or
'gri-məs   disapproval; **frown**; **scowl**

10. Freya's *grimace* after tasting the soup made clear that her
recipe had turned out (perfectly, poorly) _____ .

SENTENCE COMPLETION 1–10: Enter the required lesson
words.

---

1. The senator had _____ feelings about the proposed
law, wanting to _____ her supporters but not person-
ally favoring all the provisions.

2. The team manager's _____ told reporters that he did
not approve of the owner's latest _____ .

3. "You'll never _____ us from this legal mess," cried Ban-
ford. "Your _____ disregard for rules and regulations
will land us all in jail!"

4. The company's stock price _____**d** during the week,
rising on news of the directors' _____ actions but
falling on rumors of their misdeeds.

5. Over the years, art students have wondered about Mona Lisa's
_____ smile, thinking that perhaps Leonardo da Vinci's
painting includes a(n) _____ message.

VOCABULARY IN CONTEXT 1–10: Read the dialogue, and
on a separate sheet of paper, answer the questions that
follow. Do not repeat any of the underlined words in your
answers; use synonyms instead.

"I just can't decide what to do," Hannah said with a grimace. "I
keep fluctuating between saying yes and saying no."

"Well, do you want the job, or don't you?" her friend asked
with a benevolent smile.

"I have ambivalent feelings. I like the company, but I don't
want to move to that part of the country."

"Is there any chance the company would <u>accommodate</u> your wishes and let you split your time between there and here?"

"No. I have to make a choice. One way or the other, I have to <u>extricate</u> myself from this predicament.

1. Summarize the conversation in your own words.

2. What advice would you give Hannah to "extricate myself from this predicament"?

LESSON WORDS 11–20: Pronounce the word, spell it, study its meanings, and finish the sentence that follows it.

---

grotesque (*adj.*)   odd, distorted, or unnatural in appearance,
grō-'tesk   shape, or manner; **bizarre**; **fantastic**

11. The painting's *grotesque* images of people and animals illustrate the artist's (unimaginative, unique) _____
style.

neophyte (*n.*)   person new at something; **beginner**; **novice**; **tyro**
'nē-ə-ˌfīt

12. Because Esther is a *neophyte*, we expect her to work more
(quickly, slowly) _____ than other employees.

placard (*n.*)   notice posted in a public place; **poster**; **sign**
'pla-ˌkärd

13. One way to (inform, mislead) _____ tourists who
are visiting a historic building is to have them read a *placard*
located near the front door.

plagiarize (*v.*)   pass off (someone else's ideas or words) as one's
'plā-jə-ˌrīz   own; **steal**; **copy**

14. When it became clear that Katherine had *plagiarized* the
essay, the professor gave her a (passing, failing)
_____ grade.

precarious (*adj.*)   dependent on circumstances or chance;
pri-′ker-ē-əs   **uncertain**; **insecure**; **risky**

> 15. The climbers' (firm, unsteady) _____ footing on the
> steep slope placed them in a *precarious* situation.

solace (*n.*)   easing of sorrow, discomfort, or anxiety; **consolation**;
′sä-ləs   **comfort**

> 16. After three (hectic, relaxing) _____ weeks in the
> city, Paul sought *solace* in the quiet countryside.

synopsis (*n.*)   brief statement giving a condensation, review, or
sə-′näp-səs   outline, as of a book or play; **summary**; **abstract**

> 17. It takes (more, less) _____ time to read a literary
> work than the *synopsis*, but there is no question as to
> which approach will lead to higher grades.

translucent (*adj.*)   permitting light to pass but diffusing it so that
tran(t)s-′lü-sᵊnt   objects on the other side cannot be clearly
            seen; **lucid**; **semitransparent**

> 18. Divers found that visibility was (limited, unlimited)
> _____ in the *translucent* ocean water.

travail (*n.*)   arduous work; **toil**; **labor**
trə-′vā(ə)l

> 19. Dana felt (refreshed, exhausted) _____ after the
> day's *travail*.

waver (*v.*)   exhibit doubt or indecision; become unsteady or
′wā-vər   unsure; **vacillate**; **falter**

> 20. As the day of the match approached, Jeremy's resolve began
> to *waver*; he feared that his opponent was more (skilled,
> inexperienced) _____ than he.

SENTENCE COMPLETION 11–20: Enter the required lesson words from D, above.

1. People who lead _____ and stressful lives often find _____ in music.

2. The _____ sculpture was obviously the work of an inexperienced _____ .

3. "Here are two sure ways *not* to succeed in my class," explained the teacher: "Read the _____ instead of the actual book, and _____ other people's work when you write your papers."

4. The _____ window glass made it impossible to read the _____ mounted on the inside wall.

5. Fearing that the job would involve long hours of _____, Samantha _____**ed** in her decision to accept it.

VOCABULARY IN CONTEXT 11–20: Read the paragraph, and on a separate sheet of paper, answer the questions that follow. Do not repeat any of the underlined words in your answers; use synonyms instead.

Investing in stocks is not for the faint of heart. Neophytes are often shocked by how rapidly a company's fortunes can change. For example, buying stock in an automobile company is a precarious investment. Car buyers' tastes change. As gasoline prices rise, buyers may waver in their desire to own a large SUV. Of course, investors who do lose money in the stock market can at least find solace in the fact that they are not alone.

1. Rewrite the paragraph using your own words to paraphrase the writer's ideas.

2. Do you agree or disagree with the writer? Explain your answer.

SYNONYMS: To avoid repetition, replace the boldfaced word with a synonym from the vocabulary list below.

| falter | suit | insecure | frown | addition |
| perplexing | copy | swing | lucid | bizarre |

1. Not only is this poem a complete
   enigma to me, but I find all of this
   poet's work **enigmatic**.   1. _____

2. When you **plagiarize** even a small
   portion of another person's work,
   you are opening yourself up to charges
   of plagiarism.   2. _____

3. The hotel manager apologized for the
   inadequate accommodations and
   promised to find a room that would
   better **accommodate** our needs.   3. _____

4. Mr. Davis recently acquired a rare
   gold coin, a welcome **acquisition**
   for his extensive collection.   4. _____

5. The sight of the rough waves made
   Bill **waver** in his determination to
   go boating.   5. _____

6. The kitten was balanced precariously
   high in the tree, its grip on the branch
   precarious.   6. _____

7. The unusual weather fluctuations
   caused temperatures to **fluctuate**
   between new highs and lows.   7. _____

8. We went snorkeling in the **translucent**
   sea, the water's translucence making it
   easy to spot many colorful fish.   8. _____

9. In this comic book, the villain's evil
   experiment goes awry, leaving him with
   a **grotesque** face and a grotesquely
   deformed body.   9. _____

10. Donna grimaced when the mechanic
    handed her the bill, and her **grimace**
    told us that the repairs had been costly. 10. _____

H

ANTONYMS: In the blank space in each sentence below, enter the word most nearly the antonym of the boldfaced word. Choose your antonyms from the following list.

---

stable	opaque	malevolent	loss	expert
resolute	grin	aggravation	straightforward	attractive

1. When it comes to carpentry, Connie is a(n) _____, but her young daughter is just a **neophyte**.

2. Fans hoped that their football team's new **acquisition** would make up for the recent _____.

3. When the magic spell lifted, the **grotesque** little troll had turned into a(n) _____ child.

4. Maurice thought that he could find **solace** at his uncle's home, but he only encountered more _____.

5. The old prospector made **cryptic** comments about a hidden gold mine; we wished his clues had been more _____.

6. When soap and water successfully removed the spot from his tie, the man's **grimace** changed to a(n) _____.

7. There was so much dirt on the window pane that the once **translucent** glass was now _____.

8. At first, Tara was **ambivalent** about her career choice, but now she is _____ in pursuing her goal.

9. Management inexperience placed the new company in a **precarious** situation, but over time the business became more _____.

10. Although the country's ruler referred to himself as a **benevolent** dictator, many of his actions were clearly _____.

CONCISE WRITING: Express the thought of each sentence in NO MORE THAN FOUR WORDS.

1. Glass that is frosted allows light to come through but diffuses it, causing objects on the other side to be indistinct.

   _____

2. People engaged in politics give consideration to a large number of groups.

   _____

3. Look again at the brief statement that provides a condensation of the novel.

   _____

4. Do not ever pass off as your own ideas or words that originated with another person.

   _____

5. Clair is in search of a means of relieving the discomfort that she has been experiencing.

   _____

6. The written message that you sent seemed to have some sort of hidden significance.

   _____

VOCABULARY SKILL BUILDER

Words Derived From Other Words

Many words are formed, or _derived_, from other words by the addition of a prefix, a suffix, or both. The derived word—or _derivative_—

may or may not be the same part of speech. Recognizing derivative words, and understanding how derivatives are formed (and spelled), will help you build your vocabulary.

Nearly all the lesson words in Lesson 5 have one or more derivatives. Some of these words may be familiar to you, while others may be new. Look at the following examples. What suffixes do you recognize?

Lesson Word	Derivatives
ambivalent	ambivalence, ambivalently
brazen	brazenly, brazenness
precarious	precariously, precariousness
accommodate	accommodation, accommodative, accommodativeness, accommodator

Exercises

Each of the following lesson words has at least one derivative. On a separate sheet of paper, write the number of derivatives shown in parentheses. Use a dictionary to help you identify them. Then, for each lesson word, use one of the derivatives in a sentence.

1. benevolent (2)
2. cryptic (1)
3. grotesque (2)

4. plagiarize (3)
5. translucent (2)

 WRITING SKILL BUILDER

Organizing Content: Chronological Order

In Lesson 4 (pages 42–43), you learned how to organize content in order of importance or interest. Another organizational method is chronological order. When you use chronological order to organize a paragraph or essay, you present facts, details, examples, or a series of events in sequence according to time. Usually, you move forward in time: what happened first, what happened next, and so on. You may temporarily interrupt this sequence by inserting a flashback. Occasionally, you may find it more effective to present your content by moving backward in time.

Chronological organization is effective when you want to describe how one event leads to, or follows, another. Works of nonfiction, such as biographies and historical accounts, are typically organized in chronological order.

Activity

Choose a recent newsworthy event that occurred over a period of time, such as a space mission or a medical breakthrough. Write an essay summarizing the key developments and making clear why the event was significant. Use chronological organization for one or more of your paragraphs. In your writing, use at least two of the words that you have learned in this lesson. Write your essay on a separate sheet of paper.

LESSON 6

Lesson Preview

Some of the words that you will encounter on pages 61–63 and
64–65 of this lesson appear in bold type in the following paragraph.
Read the paragraph, and on a separate sheet of paper, answer the
questions that follow.

> Some teenagers are **intimidated** by the athletic abilities of their
> peers. These teens may become **despondent**, thinking that
> they can't measure up. However, rather than heave **plaintive**
> sighs, they should take heart. In "real" life, sports play only the
> most minor role, and academic ability and socials skills matter
> infinitely more. So don't **squander** precious time worrying
> about shooting balls through hoops or knocking them over the
> fence. Instead, focus on becoming an educated, well-rounded
> individual.

How does context—the surrounding words and sentences—help
you infer the meaning of the boldfaced words? What is the main idea
of this paragraph? Do you agree with the writer's advice? Why or
why not?

 LESSON WORDS 1–10: Pronounce the word, spell it, study
its meanings, and finish the sentence that follows it.

---

altercation (*n.*)   noisy or heated dispute; **quarrel**; **argument**
ˌȯl-tər-ˈkā-shən

  1. An *altercation* between two diners caused the restaurant
     manager to (eject, welcome) _____ both cus-
     tomers.

conspicuous (*adj.*)   attracting attention; **striking**; **noticeable**;
kən-ˈspi-kyə-wəs   **remarkable**

  2. The girl wearing the (white, red) _____coat is *con-
     spicuous* in the snowy woods.

decrepit (*adj.*)   broken down, worn out, or weakened by old age
di-'kre-pət   or long use; **feeble**; **dilapidated**; **run-down**

   3. A house in *decrepit* condition is likely to attract (many, few)
     _____ buyers.

despondent (*adj.*)   feeling discouraged, depressed, or hopeless;
di-'spän-dənt   **dejected**; **downhearted**; **despairing**

   4. Having received a twelfth (acceptance, rejection)
     _____ from publishers, the novelist became
     despondent.

enervate (*v.*)   reduce the vigor or strength of; **debilitate**; **weaken**
'e-nər-ˌvāt

   5. A hot (meal, climate) _____ may *enervate* someone
     accustomed to cool weather.

facilitate (*v.*)   make easier; help bring about; **assist**; **ease**; **aid**
fə-'si-lə-ˌtāt

   6. The use of power tools *facilitates* most (art, carpentry)
     _____ projects.

flourish (*v.*)   grow or develop with vigor; **thrive**; **prosper**
'flər-ish

   7. Once we added (fertilizer, stones) _____ to the
     garden soil, the flowers began to *flourish*.

glower (*v.*)   look or stare with anger or in a threatening way;
'glaů(-ə)r   **scowl**; **frown**

   8. The speaker *glowered* at the people in the audience who
     were (booing, applauding) _____ him.

inadvertently (*adv.*)   without intending to; **unintentionally**;
ˌi-nəd-'vər-tᵊnt-lē   **accidentally**

   9. Because I *inadvertently* wrote 7:30 instead of 6:30 on my
     desk calendar, I arrived an hour (early, late) _____
     for dinner.

intimidate (v.)   make timid or afraid, especially to influence or
in-'ti-mə-,dāt   deter by threats or violence; **frighten**; **cow**

> 10. The school bully tried to *intimidate* new students by dis-
> playing his (awards, muscles) _____ .

 SENTENCE COMPLETION 1–10: Enter the required lesson
words.

---

1. Long after their _____ had ended, the two men continued to _____ at each other.

2. The intense summer sun that helps certain garden plants
   _____ may _____ the gardener who tends
   them.

3. My _____ car looked _____ in a parking lot
   filled with much newer vehicles.

4. Carlos was _____ after he _____ ruined his
   aunt's valuable painting.

5. "I will not be _____**d** by the tactics of my opponents,"
   said the mayor. "I will do whatever I can to _____ the
   passage of this law."

VOCABULARY IN CONTEXT 1–10: Read the paragraph,
and on a separate sheet of paper, answer the questions
that follow. Do not repeat any of the underlined words in
your answers; use synonyms instead.

Last week, my neighbor and I had an unfortunate <u>altercation</u>.
Carlton objected to the battered old Mustang that I keep in my
driveway, saying that it was so <u>decrepit</u> that it was offensive to
look at. I suggested that he mind his own business, which
caused him to <u>glower</u> at me and walk off without another word.
Of course, I admit that perhaps my car is a bit <u>conspicuous</u>.
However, this is my property, and if I <u>inadvertently</u> offend Carlton with my choice of vehicles, well, I guess that's *his* problem.
I'm certainly not going to let that grouch <u>intimidate</u> me.

1. List the main idea and two supporting ideas for this paragraph.

2. How would you describe the tone of this paragraph?

3. Do you agree or disagree with the writer's position? Why?

 LESSON WORDS 11–20: Pronounce the word, spell it, study its meanings, and finish the sentence that follows it.

---

irreparable (*adj.*)   not able to be repaired, restored, or remedied;
i-'re-p(ə-)rə-bəl   **permanent**; **irreversible**

   11. The government report (praising, criticizing) _____ the governor may have done *irreparable* damage to his reelection campaign.

modification (*n.*)   limited change in something; **alteration**;
,mä-də-fə-'kā-shən   **adjustment**

   12. Adding a (comma, paragraph) _____ to this essay is a *modification* that will take only a second.

opaque (*adj.*)   not allowing light to pass through; not transparent or
ō-'pāk   translucent; **nontransparent**; **darkened**

   13. (Soot, Water) _____ on the window had left the glass nearly *opaque*.

parsimonious (*adj.*)   overly cautious with money; **stingy**; **frugal**;
,pär-sə-'mō-nē-əs   **close**

   14. Millie is so *parsimonious* that she (discards, saves) _____ torn wrapping paper.

plaintive (*adj.*)   expressing sorrow; **melancholy**; **mournful**; **sad**
'plān-tiv

   15. The dog communicated its (happiness, loneliness) _____ with a *plaintive* howl.

squander (*v.*)   spend or use extravagantly or foolishly; **waste**;
'skwän-dər   **dissipate**

16. Reggie *squanders* all his free time on (charitable, pointless)
      _____ activities.

temerity (*n.*)   reckless or foolish boldness; **rashness,**
tə-'mer-ə-tē   **foolhardiness**; **audacity**

17. Spectators were shocked because no one before had ever
had the *temerity* to (refuse, obey) _____ one of the
emperor's commands.

transition (*n.*)   passage or change from one condition, form,
tran-'zi-shən   position, place, or activity to another; **shift**;
      development; **evolution**

18. Learning to effectively organize her (time, room)
_____ helped Jayne make the *transition* from
middle school to high school.

veneer (*n.*)   thin layer of fine wood or other material used in
və-'nir   covering a surface of lesser quality; **facing**; **covering**;
      exterior

19. The wooden cabinet looked much (more, less)
_____ appealing when the *veneer* began to come
off.

zealous (*adj.*)   filled with or characterized by intense enthusiasm,
'ze-ləs   as for a cause or person; **fervent**; **passionate**

20. (Few, Thousands) _____ of the candidate's *zealous*
supporters turned out for the rally.

SENTENCE COMPLETION 11–20: Enter the required lesson words from D, above.

1. How does a person as _____ as you have the _____ to accuse anyone else of being a miser?

2. During the _____ from the old factory to the new one, workers had to make some _____s to the manufacturing process.

3. These kitchen cabinets are so old that it makes no sense to _____ any money on replacing their scratched _____.

4. People who become overly _____ in their actions can do _____ harm to their cause.

5. We heard a long, _____ howl, and through the nearly _____ fog, we could make out the indistinct shape of a wolf.

VOCABULARY IN CONTEXT 11–20: Read the paragraph, and on a separate sheet of paper, answer the questions that follow. Do not repeat any of the underlined words in your answers; use synonyms instead.

The transition from student to working adult can be a challenging one. Some people can't help but squander every paycheck on all sorts of nonessential items. A few months go by, and then they let out a plaintive moan when they realize that they haven't saved any money. Of course, you don't have to be parsimonious to accumulate savings. You do, however, have to develop sensible spending habits.

1. Paraphrase the paragraph.

2. Do you agree or disagree with the writer's advice? Explain your answer.

SYNONYMS: To avoid repetition, replace the boldfaced word with a synonym from the vocabulary list below.

striking	shift	alteration	frighten	mournful
downhearted	permanent	passionate	accidentally	prosper

1. The car manufacturer slightly modified the design of its best-selling vehicle, making several **modifications** to improve passenger safety.

1. _____**s**

2. Max, in his **conspicuous** purple jacket, arrived conspicuously late at the party.

2. _____

3. Faye expanded her flourishing business from the city into the suburbs, where the company continued to **flourish**.

3. _____

4. During the gradual **transition** from sunset to full night, the transitional period popularly known as "twilight time," motorists should drive with extra care.

4. _____

5. Leonard **inadvertently** pressed the red button, an inadvertent error that nearly shut down the entire factory.

5. _____

6. **Zealous** campaigners demonstrated their zeal by organizing rallies around the state.

6. _____

7. "We may never find our way out of this cave," Tom said despondently, beginning to feel just as **despondent** as his companions.

7. _____

8. The mechanic was not able to repair the car because the crash had done **irreparable** damage to the body of the vehicle.

8. _____

9. The judge warned the attorney not to try to **intimidate** the witness with implied threats, saying that such intimidation would not be tolerated.

9. _____

10. The dog looked up at its owner with **plaintive** eyes and then whined plaintively, as though begging her not to leave the house.

10. _____

H **ANTONYMS:** In the blank space in each sentence below, enter the word most nearly the antonym of the boldfaced word. Choose your antonyms from the following list.

---

transparent	save	inconspicuous	purposely	decline
apathetic	joyful	impede	cheerful	generous

1. Holmes is a remarkable detective, able to solve crimes not just through examination of **conspicuous** evidence but through discovery of the most _____ clues.

2. While some members of the committee do their best to **facilitate** matters, others seem to do whatever they can to _____ progress.

3. Ms. Littenger, once very _____ with her money, has become increasingly **parsimonious** as she's gotten older.

4. Gary was **despondent** after taking the difficult exam, but he became more _____ once he realized that he had done better than he thought.

5. The empire, which had long **flourished** under Malvino's rule, _____ d soon after his son became emperor.

6. At first we thought that Tina had _____ omitted Ike's name from the guest list, but then we learned that she had done so **inadvertently**.

7. The senator's nomination for president turned many _____ citizens into **zealous** voters.

8. Pulling the **opaque** shade over the _____ skylight shuts out the early morning light.

9. The songwriter's early **plaintive** ballads have gradually given way to _____ love songs.

10. Unlike his sister, who _____s a large portion of her weekly paycheck, Maury **squanders** every penny he earns.

[ ] **CONCISE WRITING:** Express the thought of each sentence in NO MORE THAN FOUR WORDS.

---

1. Plots of ground where flowers or vegetables are cultivated grow with vigor in the rays of the sun.

   _____

2. The harm that resulted from injury to property cannot be fixed or otherwise remedied.

   _____

3. The thin layer of high-quality wood that covers the rough surface has a shine to it.

   _____

4. The fact that he had lost made Hal feel extremely low in spirits.

   _____

5. People who are exceedingly careful with the money they have show good sense when they go shopping.

   _____

6. Do not spend in an extravagant or foolish manner all of the money that you have saved.

   _____

VOCABULARY SKILL BUILDER

Context Clues: Literal and Figurative Meanings

Many words have both literal and figurative meanings. The *literal* meaning of a word is its exact or usual sense. The *figurative* meaning of a word is its use in an imaginative way, for effect. You can determine which meaning the writer intends from the context in which the word is used. Compare the contexts below.

> *Literal:* The cupboard has a polished oak <u>veneer</u>.
>
> *Figurative:* Beneath his gentle <u>veneer</u>, the man is nothing but a scoundrel.
>
> *Literal:* The foolish niece <u>squandered</u> her inheritance.
>
> *Figurative:* Never <u>squander</u> an opportunity to help someone in need.

Exercises

All of the following words come from this lesson or a previous lesson. For each word, write one sentence illustrating the word's literal meaning and a second sentence showing its figurative meaning. Write your sentences on a separate sheet of paper. If you need help, check a dictionary.

diplomacy	foray	precipice	waver
embellish	torrid	flourish	opaque

WRITING SKILL BUILDER

Transitional Words and Phrases

Transitional words and phrases act as bridges between sentences or paragraphs, connecting ideas and supporting information. They typically begin a sentence, but they may also appear in the middle of a sentence or at the end. Look at the following examples.

Transitional Word or Phrase	Purpose
furthermore, also, too, in addition, as well, another, besides	To add information

Example: Jennifer plays three musical instruments. **Furthermore**, she can sing beautifully.

consequently, as a result, because of, therefore, finally, for this reason	To state an effect, result, consequence, or conclusion

Example: Owen worked harder than he ever had. **As a result**, his grades rose significantly.

however, on the other hand, but, although, even though, similarly, like, both, on the contrary, otherwise	To make a comparison or signal a change in focus or direction

Example: **Although** I love to swim in the ocean, I would not want to live along the coast.

especially, in fact, most important, above all, in particular, indeed	To add emphasis

Example: Winning the award was a joyous accomplishment for Henry. **Indeed**, it was probably the happiest moment of his life.

Activity

Recall a moment in your life that proved to be especially significant. Write an essay describing the moment and explaining its importance. Support your ideas with specific reasons, facts, details, or examples. Use transitional words and phrases to connect ideas and supporting information. In your writing, use at least two of the words that you have learned in this lesson. Write your essay on a separate sheet of paper.

LESSON 7

Lesson Preview

Some of the words that you will encounter on pages 72–74 and
75–76 of this lesson appear in bold type in the following poem. Read
the poem, and on a separate sheet of paper, answer the questions
that follow.

> Will it **detract** from my appearance
> If I dye my long hair green?
> Will people give me **baleful** stares
> And say I'm a weird-looking teen?
>
> Am I being too **impetuous**
> In making such a change?
> Will my head become so **ornate**
> That my friends think I'm strange?

What would be an appropriate title for this poem? Why do you think
the poet chose to write the poem as a series of questions?

 LESSON WORDS 1–10: Pronounce the word, spell it, study
its meanings, and finish the sentence that follows it.

---

acrid (*adj.*)   sharp, bitter, or irritating in taste or smell; **pungent**;
'a-krəd   **choking**

　　1. The *acrid* smoke coming from the grill made us all (wince,
　　　cheer) _____ .

alleviate (*v.*)   make more bearable; **relieve**; **lessen**; **ease**
ə-'lē-vē-ˌāt

　　2. The counselor's (calming, harsh) _____ words
　　　alleviated the camper's distress.

72

baleful (*adj.*)   harmful, evil, or threatening; **sinister**; **hostile**
ˈbā(ə)l-fəl

    3. The stranger's *baleful* look caused everyone in the room to take a step (forward, back) _____ .

boisterous (*adj.*)   noisy and rowdy; **high-spirited**;
ˈbȯi-st(ə-)rəs   **unrestrained**; **exuberant**

    4. Small groups of *boisterous* men and women filled the (chapel, tavern) _____ .

candor (*n.*)   frankness, honesty, or sincerity of expression;
ˈkan-ˌdȯr   **openness**; **forthrightness**

    5. We were surprised by your *candor* in (revealing, concealing) _____ the facts.

derive (*v.*)   take, receive, or obtain from a particular source or
di-ˈrīv   origin; **get**; **draw**

    6. Megan *derives* immense pleasure from her yearly visits to the (dentist, seashore) _____ .

detract (*v.*)   diminish in quality, importance, or value; take away;
di-ˈtrakt   **lessen**

    7. Several historical (facts, errors) _____ *detract* from the author's work.

emaciated (*adj.*)   abnormally or unnaturally thin; **gaunt**; **wasted**
i-ˈmā-shē-ˌā-təd

    8. Leroy's *emaciated* appearance suggested that he had been (ill, healthy) _____ .

eradicate (*v.*)   do away with completely; **eliminate**; **remove**;
i-ˈra-də-ˌkāt   **wipe out**

    9. Student volunteers offered their services to help *eradicate* (education, illiteracy) _____ in the community.

exorbitant (*adj.*)   exceeding customary, appropriate, or reasonable
ig-'zòr-bə-tənt   limits; **excessive**; **unreasonable**

> 10. If a store charges *exorbitant* prices, customers will go out of
> their way to shop (there, elsewhere) _____.

B   **SENTENCE COMPLETION 1–10**: Enter the required lesson words.

---

1. The _____ fumes coming from my old car caused
   pedestrians to give me _____ looks.

2. Tyrone's _____ face _____**ed** from his otherwise healthy appearance.

3. I appreciate your _____ concerning this matter; it helps
   to _____ my nervousness.

4. Alana _____**s** personal satisfaction from small victories;
   for example, she loves to _____ the weeds in her garden.

5. The stadium drew a large and _____ crowd, despite
   the _____ prices charged.

C   **VOCABULARY IN CONTEXT 1–10**: Read the dialogue, and
on a separate sheet of paper, answer the questions that
follow. Do not repeat any of the underlined words in your
answers; use synonyms instead.

"You look well," Berger said, trying to sound convincing. In
truth, several bouts of jungle fever had left Gómez pale and
emaciated. Berger could scarcely recognize him.

He laughed. "Your lack of candor is appreciated, old friend.
"But there is no need for concern. My years of searching have at
last achieved success." From the pocket of his tattered jacket
Gómez withdrew a well-worn map. He derived obvious pleasure
from slowly opening it and holding it up. "The treasure of
Mansu Musa," he said.

"I fear you have spent too much time in the sun," Berger said, not unkindly. He recognized Mansu Musa as the name of a ruler of a 14th-century West African empire.

"Let me <u>alleviate</u> your concerns," Gómez replied at once, reaching into another pocket. He extended his hand, displaying before Berger's astonished eyes the largest gold nugget Berger had ever seen.

1. Summarize the conversation in your own words.

2. Describe the range of reactions that Berger experiences during this brief exchange.

LESSON WORDS 11–20: Pronounce the word, spell it, study its meanings, and finish the sentence that follows it.

---

impetuous (*adj.*)   marked by impulsive action; **rash**; **hasty**
im-'pe-chə-wəs

    11. Abigail's *impetuous* nature sometimes causes her to act before (speaking, thinking) _____.

listless (*adj.*)   characterized by lack of interest or energy; **languid**; **lethargic**
'list-ləs

    12. Severe (illness, sunburn) _____ can leave you feeling *listless*.

meander (*v.*)   wander aimlessly or casually; **ramble**; **roam**
mē-'an-dər

    13. During my summer vacation, I enjoyed *meandering* through the (forest, lake) _____.

mishap (*n.*)   unfortunate accident or event; **misfortune**; **misadventure**
'mis-,hap

    14. The only *mishap* that occurred on our trip was that the airline (found, lost) _____ our luggage.

ominous (*adj.*)   foreboding evil or disaster, like a bad omen;
'ä-mə-nəs   **threatening**; **portentous**

    15. The speaker realized that he had made an (appropriate, inappropriate) _____ comment when the audience responded with *ominous* silence.

ornate (*adj.*)   elaborately or excessively decorated or ornamented;
ȯr-'nāt   **showy**; **lavish**

    16. The cabinet's *ornate* design showed that the carpenter had spent (substantial, little) _____ time working on the piece.

pretext (*n.*)   false reason or appearance intended to conceal the
'prē-,tekst   real motive or intention; **excuse**; **guise**; **ploy**

    17. Suspecting that her business partner was up to no good, Celin remained in the office (until, past) _____ closing time on the *pretext* of working late.

reiterate (*v.*)   say or do again or repeatedly; **repeat**; **restate**
rē-'i-tə-,rāt

    18. Having (previously, never) _____ given us detailed directions, the instructor *reiterated* them anyway.

succumb (*v.*)   give way; **yield**; **submit**
sə-'kəm

    19. Someone with a (weak, strong) _____ sense of morality will easily *succumb* to the temptation to do wrong.

tenet (*n.*)   principle, belief, or doctrine held to be true, as by
'te-nət   members of an organization or movement; **precept**;
        position

    20. One of the *tenets* of communism is the need to (accumulate, eliminate) _____ private property.

SENTENCE COMPLETION 11–20: Enter the required lesson words from D, above.

1. This _____ could have been avoided if you had not made such a(n) _____ decision.

2. "I will _____ my warning once more," said the park ranger. "Do not _____ into the woods, because you may get lost."

3. Ginny returned to the antique shop on the _____ of wanting to examine a(n) _____ mahogany desk.

4. Your _____ attitude suggests that you have _____**ed** to boredom.

5. "It is a(n) _____ day for democracy," declared the congressman, "when the defenders of freedom preach the _____**s** of dictatorship."

 VOCABULARY IN CONTEXT 11–20: Read the paragraph, and on a separate sheet of paper, answer the questions that follow. Do not repeat any of the underlined words in your answers; use synonyms instead.

Impetuous lad that he was, Jack began to ascend the steep slope leading to the well. Jill accompanied him, carrying a small pail. The couple meandered about the hill, despite the ominous wet patches that remained from the previous night's rainstorm. Suddenly, Jack lost his footing and fell backward, striking his head on a rock. Jill tried in vain to grab him, but instead slipped and also tumbled down. If only this foolish couple had been more careful, their mishap could easily have been prevented.

1. What is the main idea of this paragraph?

2. What well-known poem is this paragraph based on?

SYNONYMS: To avoid repetition, replace the boldfaced word with a synonym from the vocabulary list below.

hostile	wipe out	openness	showy	lethargic
repeat	threatening	rash	high-spirited	draw

1. **Candor** is a highly valued character trait, but being overly candid can hurt someone's feelings.

   1. _____

2. Many legal phrases **derive** their meaning from Latin words, although their derivation may not always be obvious.

   2. _____

3. Dark gray clouds gave the sky a(n) **ominous** appearance, and a cold wind gusted ominously.

   3. _____

4. Several days in a hospital can leave a person feeling **listless**, but cheerful visitors will help to counteract the patient's listlessness.

   4. _____

5. The **boisterous** party guests were having a wonderful time, but neighbors did not appreciate their boisterousness.

   5. _____

6. Professor Snape was determined to **reiterate** his instructions each day, and his reiterations soon became tiresome.

   6. _____

7. Tori cast a **baleful** glance in my direction, making me wonder why she was looking at me so balefully.

   7. _____

8. The **ornate** leather belt was the perfect gift for the ornately dressed actress.

   8. _____

9. **Impetuous** warriors who rush into battle may soon regret their impetuousness.

   9. _____

10. Medical researchers are working to
    eradicate various diseases,
    encouraged by the successful
    eradication of other diseases in
    the past.   10. _____

| H |

ANTONYMS: In the blank space in each sentence below, enter the word most nearly the antonym of the boldfaced word. Choose your antonyms from the following list.

---

enhance	plump	hurry	resist	worsen
calm	reasonable	measured	plain	energetic

1. The building's **ornate** entranceway contrasted sharply with its
   _____ interior.

2. Rather than react to world events in an **impetuous** manner, the
   leader of a nation must make _____ responses.

3. Plumbers who charge **exorbitant** prices will soon find their
   customers shopping around for more _____ rates.

4. Do not **succumb** to temptation! _____ the desire to
   eat that piece of chocolate cake!

5. I must be allergic to this ointment because rather than **alleviate**
   my itchy rash it _____ed it.

6. It will soon be dark, so we don't have time to **meander** along
   this trail; we need to _____.

7. His recent illness had turned the _____ Mr. Hooper
   into an **emaciated** shadow of his former self.

8. By midnight, the once **boisterous** birthday celebration had
   become decidedly _____.

9. On muggy summer days, I feel **listless**; brisk fall weather, on the
   other hand, makes me _____.

10. Rather than **detract** from your appearance, your new haircut
    _____s your looks.

CONCISE WRITING: Express the thought of each sentence in NO MORE THAN FOUR WORDS.

1. I want to convey my appreciation for the frank and honest way in which you express yourself.

   _____

2. You could have avoided the unfortunate accident that happened to you.

   _____

3. You should keep under control your tendency toward impulsive action.

   _____

4. The fees that you charge go well beyond what is appropriate or reasonable.

   _____

5. The fumes that come from acid have a sharp or irritating smell.

   _____

6. The people doing detective work made a discovery of clues that seemed to warn of evil.

   _____

J   **VOCABULARY SKILL BUILDER**

Context Clues: Synonyms and Antonyms

A synonym is a word that means the same or almost the same as another word. For example, _yield_ and _submit_ are two synonyms for *succumb.* An antonym is a word that has the opposite meaning of another word. For example, *ornate* and *simple* are antonyms.

A synonym or antonym that appears before or after an unfamiliar word can help you figure out the word's meaning. The synonym or antonym may appear in the same sentence as the unfamiliar word or in a preceding or following sentence. *Tip*: When looking for a synonym or antonym, look for a word that is the same part of speech as the unfamiliar word.

> *Example:* This chemical <u>eradicated</u> the weeds in my garden. Unfortunately, it also eliminated many of the flowers.

> *Context clue:* *Eliminated* in the second sentence is a synonym for *eradicated* in the first sentence. Note that both words are verbs.

> *Example:* The castaway had been portly before the shipwreck. When he was finally rescued, he was <u>emaciated</u>.

Context clues: *Portly* and *emaciated* are antonyms.

Exercises

Circle the synonym or antonym that can help you figure out the meaning of the underlined word. Identify the part of speech of each word pair.

1. Your advice did not <u>alleviate</u> my tension. Instead, your words only intensified the stress that I'm feeling.

2. Genevieve is an <u>impetuous</u> young lady who tends to make rash decisions.

3. The <u>acrid</u> fumes of cleaning chemicals filled the house, making us all forget the sweet smell of freshly baked apple pie that had made everyone smile that morning.

4. Equality is a prime <u>tenet</u> of democracy, an underlying principle that free people must always keep in mind.

WRITING SKILL BUILDER

Lively, Interesting Writing

To make your writing lively and interesting, vary your sentence structure. Use sentences of different lengths, and start your sentences in a variety of ways. Here are some additional tips for writing effectively.

Use active constructions.

> *Passive:* A sign was posted on the lamppost by my neighbor.

> *Active:* My neighbor posted a sign on the lamppost.

Be specific and concise.

> *Vague and wordy:* This is a great movie that really helps you see just what the Civil War was like.

> *Better:* This powerful film reveals the horrors of the Civil War through the eyes of an 18-year-old recruit.

Avoid Clichés.

> *Cliché:* We tried to stop her, but Kendra can be as stubborn as a mule

> *Better:* We tried to stop her, but once Kendra makes up her mind, a team of lawyers couldn't dissuade her.

Activity

Choose a movie that you recently viewed. It may be one that you liked or one that you disliked, but try to select a "serious" film. Write an essay explaining the filmmaker's "message" and telling whether you agree or disagree with this message, and why. Develop your essay with specific reasons, facts, details, or examples. Follow the sentence structure and word choice guidelines above to make your writing lively and interesting, and use transitional words and phrases to connect ideas and supporting information. In your essay, use at least two of the words that you have learned in this lesson. Write your essay on a separate sheet of paper.

LESSON 8

Lesson Preview

Some of the words that you will encounter on pages 83–85 and 86–87 of this lesson appear in bold type in the following paragraph. Read the paragraph, and on a separate sheet of paper, answer the questions that follow.

> I think I'd like to become an entomologist. That's a scientist who studies insects. Sure, it's an **esoteric** field that most people have probably never heard of. But I've always found it fascinating to try to **differentiate** between bees and wasps and moths and butterflies and centipedes and millipedes. No, I'm not a **fanatic** about insects. However, I do find them remarkable in many ways. For example, consider how **resilient** insects are in the face of human efforts to exterminate or control them.

What is this paragraph about? Explain how context—the surrounding words and sentences—helps you infer the meaning of the boldfaced words.

 LESSON WORDS 1–10: Pronounce the word, spell it, study its meanings, and finish the sentence that follows it.

---

affable (*adj.*)   pleasant and easy to talk to; **friendly**; **genial**
'a-fə-bəl

    1. Jamal's *affable* personality makes him (popular, unpopular) _____ with the other students.

ample (*adj.*)   generous or more than adequate in size, amount,
'am-pəl   capacity, or extent; **sufficient**; **abundant**

    2. A (small, large) _____ car usually has *ample* trunk space for luggage.

caustic (*adj.*)   cutting or sarcastic; **biting**; **scathing**
ˈkȯs-tik

  3. A *caustic* sense of humor is likely to (offend, soothe)
     _____ some people.

circumvent (*v.*)   go around; **avoid**; **evade**
ˌsər-kᵊm-ˈvent

  4. We took a (direct, roundabout) _____ route into
     town in order to *circumvent* the traffic jam.

clandestine (*adj.*)   characterized by, held in, or conducted with
klan-ˈdes-tən   secrecy; **surreptitious**; **furtive**; **secret**

  5. To safeguard their *clandestine* love affair, the couple told
     (no one, everyone) _____ about their relationship.

coherent (*adj.*)   logically ordered or connected; **consistent**;
kō-ˈhir-ənt   **sound**

  6. The attorney (convinced, confused) _____ the jury
     by presenting a *coherent* line of reasoning.

decry (*v.*)   express strong disapproval of; **condemn**; **denounce**
di-ˈkrī

  7. As a vegetarian, Desiree *decries* the eating of (steak, broccoli)
     _____ .

differentiate (*v.*)   recognize or express a difference; **distinguish**;
ˌdif-ə-ˈren(t)-shē-ˌāt   **discriminate**

  8. To grow into law-abiding adults, children must learn to *dif-
     ferentiate* between right and (wrong, left) _____
     at an early age.

diligent (*adj.*)   characterized by steady, persistent, and careful
ˈdi-lə-jənt   effort; **industrious**; **painstaking**

  9. Elias is such a *diligent* worker that he leaves the office an
     hour (earlier, later) _____ than anyone else.

disseminate (*v.*)   spread or scatter over a wide area; **distribute**;
di-ʹse-mə-ˌnāt   **broadcast; circulate**

10. (Literature, Television) _____ helps to *disseminate* information about upcoming elections.

B   **SENTENCE COMPLETION 1–10:** Enter the required lesson words.

---

1. Everyone at school likes the new student because of his _____ manner, but when it comes to expressing himself on paper, the boy has difficulty writing a(n) _____ paragraph.

2. In order to conceal our _____ relationship, we will have to _____ many obstacles.

3. The positive comments of customers provided _____ evidence of what a(n) _____ worker Wanda is.

4. Your _____ sense of humor can hurt someone's feelings. You should _____ between people who think you're funny and those who do not.

5. Some citizens _____ government secrecy; they believe that the government should _____ more information.

C   **VOCABULARY IN CONTEXT 1–10:** Read the paragraph, and on a separate sheet of paper, answer the questions that follow. Do not repeat any of the underlined words in your answers; use synonyms instead.

Ms. Vasquez is the most underlined diligent employee in the company. As part of her job, she must underlined disseminate corporate information throughout the building as rapidly as possible. She accomplishes this task flawlessly, accompanying her daily news bulletins with clearly written and underlined coherent summaries of important events. Some workers may underlined decry her occasionally underlined caustic remarks, but most praise not only her reliable job performance but also her underlined affable nature.

1. Paraphrase the paragraph.

2. If you were her employer, would this description give you
   ample reason to promote Ms. Vasquez? Why or why not?

D **LESSON WORDS 11–20:** Pronounce the word, spell it,
study its meanings, and finish the sentence that follows it.

---

esoteric (*adj.*)   intended for or understood by only a limited group
,e-sə-'ter-ik   of people; **obscure**; **abstruse**

  11. Bookstores with (extensive, limited) _____ collec-
      tions are unlikely to carry books on *esoteric* subjects.

fanatic (*n.*)   person whose devotion to a cause, belief, or activity is
fə-'na-tik   excessive or beyond reason; **zealot**; **extremist**

  12. Lori is a *fanatic* about exercise, working out (two, seven)
      _____ days a week.

fraudulent (*adj.*)   characterized by, based on, or achieved by
'frò-jə-lənt   fraud; **deceitful**; **dishonest**

  13. Authorities will (investigate, reward) _____ anyone
      suspected of making *fraudulent* insurance claims.

hinder (*v.*)   make slow or difficult; hold back; **impede**; **hamper**
'hin-der

  14. The roadway's (slippery, paved) _____ surface *hin-*
      dered the movement of vehicles.

inimitable (*adj.*)   not capable of being imitated or copied;
,i-'ni-mə-tə-bəl   **matchless**; **unique**

  15. Other artists have (managed, failed) _____ to dupli-
      cate this painter's *inimitable* style.

ludicrous (*adj.*)   amusing through absurdity or exaggeration;
ˈlü-də-krəs   **ridiculous**; **laughable**; **preposterous**

    16. Mr. Johnson's suggestion was so *ludicrous* that some members of the committee began to (giggle, applaud) _____.

malevolence (*n.*)   intense, often vicious ill will; **malice**; **hatred**;
mə-ˈle-və-lən(t)s   **spite**

    17. The relentless *malevolence* of the movie's (hero, villain) _____ added tension to the plot.

partition (*n.*)   something that divides, such as a wall; **divider**;
pär-ˈti-shən   **barrier**

    18. A curtain serves as the *partition* that (separates, joins) _____ the two sections of the seating area.

prolific (*adj.*)   highly productive or inventive; **creative**; **fruitful**
prə-ˈli-fik

    19. My favorite author is quite *prolific*, so it has taken me (weeks, years) _____ to read all of her works.

resilient (*adj.*)   tending to recover from or adjust easily to
ri-ˈzil-yənt   adversity; **buoyant**; **hardy**

    20. A *resilient* person is likely to view a setback as (temporary, permanent) _____.

E   **SENTENCE COMPLETION 11–20:** Enter the required lesson words from D, above.

---

1. It's no wonder that land investors greeted the salesman with _____: it turned out that the deed was _____.

2. Customers praise the designer's _____ technique, but they consider his exorbitant prices to be _____.

3. As a lover of poetry, Higgins is a(n) _____; she is also the most _____ poet I know.

4. Construction of the highway divider that would serve as a roadway _____ temporarily _____**ed** the flow of
traffic.

5. The _____ inscription on the stone tablet described
how _____ these ancient people were when facing
natural disaster.

VOCABULARY IN CONTEXT 11–20: Read the dialogue,
and on a separate sheet of paper, answer the questions
that follow. Do not repeat any of the underlined words in
your answers; use synonyms instead.

"That is the most <u>ludicrous</u> idea I've ever heard!" said Gladys.
"You can't build a <u>partition</u> across this room."

"Why not?" said Abe, unable to understand his wife's reluctance.

"Because it's our *living room. That's* why not!"

"Well, we can 'live' in half of it, and I can use the other half as
my study."

Gladys eyed her husband with a touch of <u>malevolence</u>. "Why
would you need a study?"

"So I can write a novel."

"You've never written anything in your life."

"Lack of privacy <u>hinders</u> my creativity. If I had my own study,
I could become quite a <u>prolific</u> writer."

1. Summarize the conversation in your own words.

2. Do you think Abe's idea is reasonable? Why or why not?

SYNONYMS: To avoid repetition, replace the boldfaced word with a synonym from the vocabulary list below.

secret	sound	impede	hardy	friendly
biting	industrious	extremist	ridiculous	malice

1. Hal arrived at the party wearing a **ludicrous** outfit, and everyone immediately asked why he was dressed so ludicrously.

1. _____

2. Tracy is a(n) **affable** woman who smiles affably and says good morning to everyone she meets.

2. _____

3. Shrubs must be **resilient** to survive in this climate, and this year's weather severely tested their resilience.

3. _____

4. Raphael is a(n) **fanatic** whose fanatical behavior sometimes alarms others.

4. _____

5. When she is in a sour mood, Jan speaks caustically to everyone, but she seems to save her most **caustic** comments for me.

5. _____

6. Telephone calls **hinder** my work because they interrupt my thinking. The telephone can be such a hindrance sometimes.

6. _____

7. The **clandestine** meeting took place at midnight, with all of the participants arriving clandestinely on foot, wearing disguises.

7. _____

8. The evil scientist, his eyes shining with **malevolence**, gave his victim a malevolent grin.

8. _____

9. The lawyer tried to present **coherent** arguments, but several jurors thought that the case lacked coherence.

9. _____

10. **Diligent** students typically earn high grades, while those who show less diligence do not do as well.

10. _____

H **ANTONYMS:** In the blank space in each sentence below, enter the word most nearly the antonym of the boldfaced word. Choose your antonyms from the following list.

unfriendly	insufficient	facilitate	ordinary	illogical
praise	lazy	genuine	unproductive	sensible

1. Rather than **hinder** our progress with your objections, why not make suggestions that will _____ the project?

2. Theo may not be the company's most **diligent** employee, but he is by no means _____.

3. Even though your reasoning is **coherent**, your conclusion is _____.

4. The comedian's **inimitable** style sets him apart from more _____ performers.

5. Gerald has an **affable** nature, very different from that of his _____ older brother.

6. This composer, so _____ in her youth, became increasingly **prolific** in later life.

7. While some **decry** the emphasis on violence in video games, others _____ the excitement.

8. The bill was **ludicrous** in its original form, but Congress ultimately passed a more _____ version of the law.

9. I thought that we brought **ample** money for our trip, but it turns out that our funds are _____.

10. Although this document may look **fraudulent**, I can assure you it is _____.

| | **CONCISE WRITING:** Express the thought of each sentence in NO MORE THAN FOUR WORDS. |

1. Daily papers containing news spread information over a wide area.

   _____

2. I am fascinated by books that are written specifically for only a very limited number of people.

   _____

3. Watch out for people whose commitment to a political cause goes beyond the boundaries of good sense.

   _____

4. The quantity of supplies that we have with us is more than adequate.

   _____

5. People who pay others to work for them place high value on employed workers who show persistent and careful effort.

   _____

6. People with the ability to recover from adverse events are able to surmount difficulties they encounter.

   _____

VOCABULARY SKILL BUILDER

Word Parts: Prefixes, Suffixes, and Roots

In Lessons 3 and 4 (pages 30–31 and 42), you learned the meaning of a number of prefixes, suffixes, and roots. Here are some others. Most of the examples are vocabulary words or synonyms that appeared in this lesson or in a previous lesson. What other examples can you think of?

Prefix	Meaning	Example
ex-	"out" or "away"	extricate
ir-	"not" or "the opposite of"	irreparable
re-	"back" or "again"	restate
trans-	"through" or "across"	transition

Suffix	Meaning	Example
-ate, -en, -ize	"make" or "cause to be"	debilitate, lessen, idolize
-ness	"quality or condition of being"	foolhardiness

Root	Meaning	Example
ject	"throw"	inject
ten	"hold" or "keep"	tenacious

Exercises

Each of the following words appears as a lesson word or a synonym in this lesson or in a previous lesson. Circle the prefixes and suffixes, and underline the roots, in these words. Then, on a separate sheet of paper, use each word in a sentence. You may use more than one word in the same sentence. If you need help, check a dictionary.

1. facilitate
2. dejected
3. irreversible
4. reiterate
5. translucent
6. exterior
7. rashness
8. reconcile
9. tenet

WRITING SKILL BUILDER

The Importance of Essay Planning

Much of the work required to develop an effective essay should take place *before* writing. Start by brainstorming ideas, and then plan and outline your content and organization. Many students find it beneficial to make a visual plan, such as a diagram or word web, to help them shape their essay. Keep in mind that the effort that you invest in *prewriting* will make writing the first draft much easier.

Activity

People should be far more concerned with finding employment that they enjoy than with finding jobs that pay well. Do you agree or disagree with this statement? Why?

Plan and write an essay expressing your point of view. Include an introduction, body, and conclusion. Be sure that your essay has a clear central idea and that every paragraph relates to this idea. Support your position with specific reasons, facts, details, or examples, and use transitional words and phrases to connect your ideas and supporting information. In your essay, use at least two of the words that you have learned in this lesson. Write your essay on a separate sheet of paper.

Unit II Review and Enrichment

 CLOSE READING: Read the following statements. Then answer questions 1–10.

STATEMENTS

The kitten became so tangled up in the yarn that it took Sheila five minutes to free her.

Francisco considered copying someone else's research paper but then concluded that would be wrong.

The Pober family contributes to five different charities and also does volunteer work at the local homeless shelter.

The dispute between Dave and Rick grew so loud that the coach had to separate them.

When Lefty Boyd struck him out for the third time, Tony gave the pitcher a furious look.

No one was a more passionate fan than Eliza, who attended every concert that the band gave within 200 miles of her home and started a local fan club.

While cleaning the gutters, Rollins slipped off the ladder and sprained his ankle.

Androcles gently removed the thorn from the lion's foot, a good deed that would later be repaid.

Clark and Louis were both arrested for attempting to pass out counterfeit twenty-dollar bills.

Somehow, Gwen managed to write four novels in a single year, although none of them impressed publishers.

QUESTIONS

1. Who had a mishap? _____

2. Who became involved in an altercation? _____

3. Who was zealous? _____

4. Who was extricated? _____

5. Who alleviated discomfort? _____

6. Who engaged in fraudulent activity? _____

7. Who was glowered at? _____

8. Who is benevolent? _____

9. Who was prolific? _____

10. Who decided not to plagiarize? _____

B **CONCISE WRITING:** Make the following passages more concise using no more than the number of words suggested.

---

1. The intense ill will that you show does not make me afraid. As a matter of fact, it strikes me as amusing because of its absurdity. *(Cut to about 12–15 words.)*

---

2. It was very hard to recognize any person through the dark glass, which barely allowed light to pass through it, but since Duncan was such a big person, he stood out and attracted attention. *(Cut to about 20–24 words.)*

---

3. The mansion was old and broken down, and all around it stood sculptures made of stone that appeared distorted in shape, giving the property a feeling that evil or disaster would soon occur. *(Cut to about 17–20 words.)*

_____

_____

4. My hope had been to use this spray, which has a sharp and bitter odor, to completely do away with all of the bugs inhabiting my home, but the insects turned out to have a better ability to recover than I figured they would. *(Cut to about 23–26 words.)*

_____

_____

5. Most of the time I'm the kind of person who works steadily and carefully, but it's spring and it's a warm day, and I just don't feel like working on anything. Therefore, I have made the decision that I am going to wander aimlessly all around the park. *(Cut to about 23–26 words.)*

_____

_____

_____

C **CLOSE READING:** Read the following statements. Then answer questions 11–20.

STATEMENTS

Everyone adores Mrs. Finnegan. In fact, students voted her the school's most popular teacher.

The museum purchased a Rodin sculpture, a welcome addition to the growing collection.

"Midnight," whispered the woman in black. "At the old pier. Come alone, and tell no one. Make sure you're not followed."

"Well, it's a lovely car," Ms. Reynolds agreed, "but I fear that I've paid way too much for it. I wish I had shopped around more."

When Diana lifted the receiver, she heard a chilling voice whisper, "Seven days . . ." Then the line went dead.

Lonye spent all of her contest prize winnings in just three days, buying clothing that she didn't really need.

"Forgive me for saying so," Kyle said, "but to tell you the truth, this is the worst meat loaf I've ever tasted!"

Feeling stressed after a difficult week at work, Gordon spent Saturday hiking through the woods.

When the pipe burst and the basement flooded, Dennis's treadmill was damaged beyond repair.

In support of their candidate, the group of students handed out leaflets throughout the town.

QUESTIONS

11. Who arranged a clandestine meeting? _____

12. Who found solace? _____

13. Who received an ominous phone call? _____

14. Who squandered money? _____

15. Who made an acquisition? _____

16. Who disseminated information? _____

17. Who was charged an exorbitant price? _____

18. Who owns something irreparable? _____

19. Who displayed too much candor? _____

20. Who is affable? _____

ANALOGIES: Which lettered pair of words—a, b, c, d, or e—most nearly has the same relationship as the numbered pair? Enter the letter of your answer in the space provided.

1. INJURY : GRIMACE
   - a. dispute: opinion
   - b. accident : mishap
   - c. novel : synopsis
   - d. smile : happiness
   - e. victory : cheer

   1. _____

2. REASONABLE : EXORBITANT
   - a. boisterous : exuberant
   - b. gentle : caustic
   - c. precarious : alarming
   - d. cryptic : enigmatic
   - e. logical : coherent

   2. _____

3. ZEALOUS : FANATIC
   - a. indifferent : voter
   - b. enigmatic : solution
   - c. parsimonious : miser
   - d. impetuous : temperament
   - e. professional : neophyte

   3. _____

4. OBSTACLE : CIRCUMVENT
   - a. temptation : succumb
   - b. colors : differentiate
   - c. money : squander
   - d. resistance : overcome
   - e. information : disseminate

   4. _____

5. ANGER : GLOWER
   - a. temerity : listen
   - b. malevolence : forgive
   - c. grief : weep
   - d. candor : deceive
   - e. anticipation : scowl

   5. _____

VOCABULARY SKILL BUILDER

Do the following exercises on a separate sheet of paper.

1. Each of the following lesson words has at least two derivatives. Write the derivatives, using a dictionary as needed to help you identify them. Then, for each lesson word, use one of the derivatives in a sentence. (You can form a derivative by changing a word's ending.)

   a. intimidate   b. plaintive   c. transition

2. For each of the following words, write one sentence illustrating the word's literal meaning and a second sentence showing its figurative meaning. If you need help, check a dictionary.

   a. circumvent   b. impasse   c. caustic

3. Circle the synonym or antonym that can help you figure out the meaning of the underlined word. Identify the part of speech of each word pair.

   a. There is <u>ample</u> room in the closet for your sports equipment. In fact, there is sufficient space for mine as well.

   b. Beth says that she <u>inadvertently</u> knocked over the vase, but I think she did it deliberately.

   c. The storeroom window, once <u>translucent</u>, is now so dirt covered that it has become opaque.

4. Circle the prefixes and suffixes, and underline the roots, in these words. Then use each word in a sentence. You may use more than one word in the same sentence. If you need help, check a dictionary.

   a. irresponsibleness   b. rejection   c. tenable

Cumulative Review
for Units I and II

A Circle the word that best completes each sentence.

1. Daytime temperatures often _____ during the spring.

   a. fluctuate   b. circumvent   c. castigate   d. aspire

2. "This is a quiet little inn," said the manager, "so we discourage _____ behavior."

   a. fastidious   b. boisterous   c. ingenuous   d. emaciated

3. I can _____ no difference between your point of view and hers.

   a. reiterate   b. incite   c. discern   d. alleviate

4. Watching "reality" television shows is about the worst way I can think of to _____ free time.

   a. exculpate   b. espouse   c. squander   d. surmise

5. Do not _____ my report. Do your own research!

   a. impart   b. scrutinize   c. extricate   d. plagiarize

6. Gil left the party early on the _____ of having to walk his dog.

   a. pretext   b. solace   c. valise   d. anecdote

7. Brittany enjoys cooking, but baking is her _____.

   a. artifice   b. subterfuge   c. banter   d. forte

8. If you continue to talk on your cell phone while driving, it is _____ that you will have a car crash.

   a. inevitable   b. precarious   c. parsimonious   d. insipid

9. The two small offices were separated by nothing more than a thin metal _____.

   a. tenet   b. tome   c. ultimatum   d. partition

10. Your _____ expression suggests that you do not under-stand how to solve this algebra problem.

    a. pretentious   b. quizzical   c. gratuitous   d. squalid

B Circle the correct synonym for each underlined word.

11. a fastidious dresser
    a. bashful b. proficient c. genial d. fussy

12. a petulant temperament
    a. frugal b. peevish c. lethargic d. lavish

13. incite a riot
    a. evade b. reconcile c. simulate d. provoke

14. enigmatic symbols
    a. mystifying b. hostile c. erroneous d. garrulous

15. hold a placard
    a. divider b. suitcase c. sign d. rendezvous

16. scrutinize a contract
    a. denounce b. study c. exonerate d. enhance

17. grotesque images
    a. obscure b. offensive c. bland d. bizarre

18. intimidate a person
    a. debilitate b. scold c. frighten d. infuriate

19. look for solace
    a. insight b. complexity c. consolation d. forthrightness

20. facilitate a process
    a. assist b. copy c. circulate d. dissipate

LESSON 9

Lesson Preview

Some of the words that you will encounter on pages 102–104 and 105–106 of this lesson appear in bold type in the following poem. Read the poem, and on a separate sheet of paper, answer the questions that follow.

> You are an **atrocious** liar—
> I know that unicorns are not real.
> And your photo that **depicts** one
> Is a **hoax** that you cannot conceal.
>
> So take your phony picture elsewhere—
> This newspaper would never buy it.
> To **deviate** from the truth is reckless,
> And I'm surprised you'd even try it!

Who is the speaker in this poem? Who is the listener? What is this poem about?

 LESSON WORDS 1–10: Pronounce the word, spell it, study its meanings, and finish the sentence that follows it.

adverse (*adj.*)   not favorable; **harmful**; **unfavorable**;
ad-'vers   **undesirable**

  1. Eating (fatty, nutritious) _____ foods can have an
     adverse effect on your health.

atrocious (*adj.*)   very bad, unpleasant, or offensive; **appalling**;
ə-'trō-shəs   **outrageous**; **dreadful**

  2. The student's (meticulous, illegible) _____ hand-
     writing is *atrocious*.

102

banal (*adj.*)   not original, fresh, or new; **trite**; **commonplace**
bə-'nal

   3. The *banal* plot of this novel is typical of the author's (inimitable, unimaginative) _____ fiction.

belligerent (*adj.*)   inclined to fight; **quarrelsome**; **hostile**;
bə-'li-jə-rent   **aggressive**

   4. If you continue to make *belligerent* comments, we are (likely, unlikely) _____ to have an argument.

calamity (*n.*)   disastrous event bringing about severe loss and
kə-'la-mə-tē   suffering; great misfortune; **catastrophe**; **disaster**

   5. The (construction, collapse) _____ of the dam proved to be a *calamity* for nearby towns.

component (*n.*)   constituent part; **ingredient**; **element**
kəm-'pō-nənt

   6. A high-quality display monitor is a key *component* of a (computer, stereo) _____ system.

depict (*v.*)   represent by or as if by drawing or painting; **portray**;
di-'pikt   **show**

   7. This dramatic (symphony, mural) _____ *depicts* Tenochtitlán, the beautiful capital city of the Aztec Empire.

designate (*v.*)   indicate or select for a particular purpose, duty, or
'de-zig-ˌnāt   office; **specify**; **appoint**; **assign**

   8. Committee members voted to *designate* Ms. Seymour as their (resident, representative) _____ for the convention.

deviate (*v.*)   depart or turn aside (from a course, direction,
'dē-vē-ˌāt   standard, topic, or the like); **diverge**; **stray**

   9. Our flight was forced to *deviate* from its usual route because of the (inclement, pleasant) _____ weather.

elucidate (*v.*)   make clear; explain; **clarify**; **explicate**
i-'lü-sə-ˌdāt

   10. "Since you feel (certain, confused) _____ about the
       meaning of this passage," said the professor, "I will
       elucidate."

B **SENTENCE COMPLETION 1–10:** Enter the required lesson
   words.

---

1. Even though it is a(n) _____ story, the author does have
   a unique way of _____**ing** characters.

2. In her effort to _____ the text, the teacher
   _____**d** from the standard interpretation.

3. Unless the nations of the world abandon their _____
   ways, the result may be a global _____.

4. The family _____**d** Dad to select and purchase the
   stereo _____**s**.

5. Any medicine with such a(n) _____ taste is sure to have
   _____ side effects.

C **VOCABULARY IN CONTEXT 1–10:** Read the paragraph,
   and on a separate sheet of paper, answer the questions
   that follow. Do not repeat any of the underlined words in
   your answers; use synonyms instead.

Kranshaw was the most belligerent man on the block. Most people went out of their way to avoid their unpleasant neighbor.
However, this was all but impossible for the Bronson family,
since their house was next door to his. When the huge oak
tree in Kranshaw's backyard began to lean dangerously toward
their home, the Bronsons realized that they would have to
confront their quarrelsome neighbor in order to avoid a possible calamity. No one volunteered, of course, so the family
designated Mrs. Bronson to talk to Kranshaw. It would be her

task to <u>depict</u> the risks of the situation as calmly, but convincingly, as she could.

1. Paraphrase the paragraph.

2. If you were Mrs. Bronson, how would you approach Kranshaw?

LESSON WORDS 11–20: Pronounce the word, spell it, study its meanings, and finish the sentence that follows it.

---

exasperate (*v.*)   irritate or annoy greatly; make angry; **infuriate**;
ig-'zas-pə-,rāt   **aggravate**

11. Leon's parents found his habit of cracking his knuckles *exasperating* and asked him to (continue, stop) _____.

flippant (*adj.*)   lacking proper respect or seriousness;
'fli-pənt   **disrespectful; frivolous**

12. The sergeant was (pleased, displeased) _____ with the private's *flippant* reply to his question.

heirloom (*n.*)   possession of special meaning or value that is passed
'er-,lüm   on from one generation to the next; **inheritance**;
    antique; hand-me-down

13. This lovely gold locket, a family *heirloom*, was a gift from my (grandmother, daughter) _____.

hoax (*n.*)   act intended to deceive; **deception; fraud**
'hōks

14. The radio program describing the arrival of (Martians, Californians) _____ in New Jersey proved to be a *hoax*.

impediment (*n.*)   something that impedes or hampers; **obstacle**;
im-'pe-də-mənt   **hindrance**

15. The main *impediment* to settlement of the dispute was the strikers' (eagerness, reluctance) _____ to compromise.

lurid (*adj.*)   causing shock, horror, or revulsion; **terrible**;
'lûr-əd   **startling; sensational**

16. The defendant was convicted and sentenced to twenty
(days, years) _____ in prison for her *lurid* crimes.

pedestal (*n.*)   base, stand, or other supporting structure; **support**;
'pe-dəs-t'l   **foundation**

17. A marble bust of Aristotle stood (atop, beneath)
_____ the stone *pedestal*.

tacit (*adj.*)   implied or expressed without being openly
'ta-sət   communicated; **unspoken; implicit**

18. Cindy interpreted her parents' (silence, go-ahead)
_____ as *tacit* approval of her request.

terminate (*v.*)   bring to an end; **conclude; stop; finish**
'tər-mə-nāt

19. Jacob's (exceptional, inadequate) _____ job performance caused the manager to *terminate* his employment
with the company.

vehemently (*adv.*)   in a manner showing strong or intense feeling;
'vē-ə-mənt-lē   **forcefully; passionately**

20. The (whispers, shouts) _____ of the audience
made clear that they were *vehemently* opposed to the
president's position on the issue.

E   **SENTENCE COMPLETION 11–20:** Enter the required
lesson words from D, above.

---

1. When Mr. Costello discovered that his associate had perpetrated
a(n) _____, he _____**d** their partnership
immediately.

2. Ms. Digby was _____**d** when she realized that she had
encountered yet another _____ to her plan.

3. "Rather than listening to any more of your _____ comments about my proposal," the councilman told his assistant, "I would prefer your _____ disapproval."

4. The jade statue is a 150-year-old _____, but the _____ on which it stands is much newer.

5. Neighbors objected to the _____ mural and _____ demanded its removal.

F   **VOCABULARY IN CONTEXT 11–20:** Read the paragraph, and on a separate sheet of paper, answer the questions that follow. Do not repeat any of the underlined words in your answers; use synonyms instead.

Many e-mail messages are nothing more than <u>hoaxes</u> designed to fool gullible people. In fact, computer users are becoming increasingly <u>exasperated</u> by the large quantity of deceptive messages they receive. Users <u>vehemently</u> denounce the senders of such messages, as well as those who fill e-mail boxes with junk mail and <u>lurid</u> advertisements of distasteful products. Some users are so fed up that they are tempted to <u>terminate</u> their Internet service.

1. Paraphrase the paragraph.

2. In what ways is junk e-mail an <u>impediment</u> to Internet use?

G   **SYNONYMS:** To avoid repetition, replace the boldfaced word with a synonym from the vocabulary list below.

---

show	appoint	disaster	unfavorable	appalling
hindrance	antique	infuriate	startling	stop

1. Having survived great adversity in the past, the Robinson family feels confident that they can overcome their current **adverse** circumstances.   1. _____

2. Construction of a new ramp will be a(n) **impediment** during rush hour, because it will impede the flow of highway traffic.

2. _____

3. The artist's depiction of our small town is true to life, except that she **depicts** an unrealistic number of cars on the main street.

3. _____**s**

4. The house is filled with priceless **heirlooms**, which Cynthia plans to pass on to her favorite heir.

4. _____**s**

5. It was an **atrocious** crime that shocked the nation. Citizens demanded that the criminal be severely punished for committing such an atrocity.

5. _____

6. The paperback's luridly drawn cover made me gasp; never before had I seen such a **lurid** picture on a book.

6. _____

7. Mr. Schuyler has officially **terminated** his relationship with this bank. The termination takes effect immediately.

7. _____**ed**

8. The week's calamitous events—a flood, a bridge collapse, and then a fire— stunned local residents. Each **calamity** was worse than the one before.

8. _____

9. Juan's designation as captain surprised the team. Everyone had thought that the coach would **designate** one of the more experienced players.

9. _____

10. Your exasperating habit of arriving late for every appointment **exasperates** me.

10. _____**s**

ANTONYMS: In the blank space in each sentence below, enter the word most nearly the antonym of the boldfaced word. Choose your antonyms from the following list.

positive	launch	excellent	explicit	keep to
incentive	agreeable	original	serious	engaging

1. Manuel is such a(n) _____ young man, quite different from his **belligerent** uncle.

2. The author followed her first novel, a **banal** tale of young love, with a much more _____ work.

3. Rising interest rates can be an **impediment** to home buyers, while falling rates can be a(n) _____.

4. In its early years, this vehicle's safety record was **atrocious**, but in the most recent tests the car's performance was _____.

5. You need to understand that there is a time and place to be _____, not **flippant**.

6. During the debate, neither candidate chose to **deviate** from his party's official position. Both were determined to _____ the party line.

7. The accused man's silence appeared to be a **tacit** admission of guilt, but the prosecutor needed _____ evidence.

8. The proposed law is sure to have an **adverse** impact on the environment. We hope that it will be amended to bring about more _____ results.

9. We plan to _____ this project in January and **terminate** it at the end of the year.

10. The writer's **lurid** description of events contrasted sharply with the oddly _____ photographs.

CONCISE WRITING: Express the thought of each sentence in NO MORE THAN FOUR WORDS.

1. The brief story you told that is supposed to be amusing offends me.

    _____

2. Hannah indicated her favorable opinion without actually saying anything.

    _____

3. Body movements that suggest an inclination to fight are offensive to various individuals.

    _____

4. An extreme scarcity of food is a disastrous event that causes great suffering.

    _____

5. Treat as highly valued objects those possessions of your family that are passed on from generation to generation.

    _____

6. People who favor capitalism express strong opposition to economic systems based on the elimination of private property.

    _____

[J]   **VOCABULARY SKILL BUILDER**

Shades of Meaning

The *denotation* of a word is its literal or exact meaning. Many words also have a *connotation*—an implied or suggested meaning. The connotation may be positive or negative, favorable or unfavorable. Sometimes it's just a slightly different shade of meaning.

By choosing words with a particular connotation, writers can slant text in one direction or another. For example, compare the following sentences. Even though the underlined words have similar denotations, their connotations are different. How does this difference in connotation affect the sentences? What does it suggest about the feelings of the writer?

Positive connotation: The city should get these <u>homeless</u> <u>pups</u> off the street.

Negative connotation: The city should get these <u>stray</u> <u>mutts</u> off the street.

Neutral: An <u>eager</u> <u>crowd</u> of reporters was waiting outside.

Negative connotation: An <u>impatient</u> <u>mob</u> of reporters was waiting outside.

Exercises

For each pair of synonyms below, first write the denotation that the words have in common. Then explain how the words differ in connotation. All of these words come from this lesson or previous lessons. Write your answers on a separate sheet of paper. If you need help, check a dictionary.

1. forcefully, passionately
2. uncertain, conflicted
3. kindly, generous
4. shameless, impudent
5. vacillate, falter
6. sinister, hostile
7. offensive, detestable
8. unjustified, unnecessary

 WRITING SKILL BUILDER

Accomplishing Your Purpose

As you plan and write an essay, keep your writing purpose—your reason for writing—clearly in focus. Is your primary purpose to persuade your reader? To explain a concept or process? To tell a story?

To describe a person or place? Organize your essay in the most effective way to accomplish your purpose, and select your words with care. As you saw in the preceding *Vocabulary Skill Builder,* you can slant and shape writing through your choice of language.

Activity

Plan and write a *persuasive* essay on a topic of your choice. Be sure that your essay has a clear central idea and that every paragraph relates to this idea. Develop your essay with specific supporting information—reasons, facts, details, or examples. Choose words and phrases whose connotation helps to convey your meaning and purpose. In your essay, use at least two of the words that you have learned in this lesson. Write your essay on a separate sheet of paper.

LESSON 10

Some of the words that you will encounter on pages 113–115 and 116–117 of this lesson appear in bold type in the following paragraph. Read the paragraph, and on a separate sheet of paper, answer the questions that follow.

> **Equitable** resolution of a disagreement requires calm discussion and negotiation. There is no point in **haranguing** the other person with your point of view, because shouting only provokes negative feelings. Better to soothe the other person's **ire** by offering to compromise. Remember, too, that once you make a statement, you cannot **retract** it. So before you speak, try to **assess** the impact of what you are about to say.

How does context help you infer the meaning of the boldfaced words? What is the main idea of the paragraph? Do you think the writer's advice is sound? Why or why not?

 LESSON WORDS 1–10: Pronounce the word, spell it, study its meanings, and finish the sentence that follows it.

---

assess (*v.*)   determine or estimate the value, amount, effect, or
ə-'ses   importance of; **evaluate**; **consider**

  1. After the factory was flooded, (electricians, photographers)
  _____ *assessed* the damage.

austere (*adj.*)   having a stern and cold appearance or manner;
ȯ-'stir   **severe**; **harsh**

  2. Young children (adore, fear) _____ Mr. Lorenz
  because he seems so *austere*.

113

clairvoyant (*adj.*)   supposedly able to see or know things that are
kler-'vói-ənt   beyond the range of ordinary perception;
            psychic; telepathic; extrasensory

    3. Madame DeFarge claims to have *clairvoyant* powers,
enabling her to communicate with the (living, dead)
_____.

deficient (*adj.*)   not adequate; **lacking; insufficient**
di-'fi-shənt

    4. If you (eat, avoid) _____ fruits and vegetables, your
diet may be *deficient* in vitamins.

discord (*n.*)   lack of agreement or harmony; **disagreement;**
'dis-,kórd   **conflict**

    5. *Discord* among club members leads to many (agreements,
arguments) _____.

duplicity (*n.*)   concealing one's true intentions through deceptive
dù-'pli-sə-tē   actions or words; **deceitfulness; treachery**

    6. Because of your past *duplicity*, we find it (easy, difficult)
_____ to trust you.

eccentric (*adj.*)   deviating from the usual or conventional, as in
ik-'sen-trik   manner, appearance, or behavior; **odd;**
            peculiar; unconventional

    7. Yuda's *eccentric* nature makes his actions (predictable,
unpredictable) _____.

epigram (*n.*)   concise saying that is wise or witty; **witticism;**
'e-pə-,gram   **axiom**

    8. Readers gain (insight, wealth) _____ from the *epi-
grams* that appear in Benjamin Franklin's *Poor Richard's
Almanac.*

equitable (*adj.*)   dealing justly and equally with everyone
'e-kwə-tə-bəl   concerned; **fair; just**

    9. The *equitable* settlement of a dispute is likely to (satisfy, dis-
please) _____ both sides.

harangue (v.)   address with a long, noisy speech, usually for the
hə-'raŋ   purpose of scolding or instructing; **berate**;
                      upbraid

   10. The coach *harangued* team members for their (careless,
      excellent) _____ play.

SENTENCE COMPLETION 1–10: Enter the required lesson words.

---

1. Mr. Tyler is a(n) _____ teacher, who likes to dress up
   like William Shakespeare, climb up on a chair, and
   _____ students about the need to read more plays.

2. "I don't have to be _____ to know that you're talking
   behind my back," said Ginny. "Your _____ is obvious!"

3. The lawyer began her speech with a memorable
   _____: "Justice delayed is justice denied"; then
   she went on to discuss the need for _____ solutions
   to difficult legal problems.

4. This test will _____ your math skills and help to determine whether you are _____ in any areas.

5. It was clear from the _____ looks of the members that
   the committee was still racked by _____.

VOCABULARY IN CONTEXT 1–10: Read the paragraph,
and on a separate sheet of paper, answer the questions
that follow. Do not repeat any of the underlined words in
your answers; use synonyms instead.

There's no one quite like my Aunt Sally. To say that she is
eccentric is something of an understatement. She has more odd
traits than anyone I've ever met. For instance, she's always
inventing her own epigrams that don't quite make sense. "A
sleeping cat tells no lies" is one of her favorites. Sally also insists
that she is clairvoyant, though as far as anyone can remember,

she has never demonstrated any such powers. My Dad says that someone ought to <u>assess</u> Sally's sanity, but he's only kidding. I think.

1. Describe Sally in your own words.

2. How does the narrator feel about Sally? What makes you think so?

D **LESSON WORDS 11–20:** Pronounce the word, spell it, study its meanings, and finish the sentence that follows it.

---

ire (*n.*)   intense anger; **wrath**; **rage**
'īr

    11. Matthew risked the *ire* of hometown fans by cheering for the (opposing, home) _____ team.

itinerary (*n.*)   route, or proposed outline, of a journey; **travel**
ī-'ti-nə-,rer-ē   **plan**; **schedule**

    12. Ms. Lawrence is planning to (phone, visit) _____ friends in four Chinese cities next month, but Beijing is not on her *itinerary*.

jargon (*n.*)   specialized language of a particular group, profession,
'jär-gən   or field; **terminology**; **lingo**

    13. Making sense of legal *jargon* is a task best left to (teachers, attorneys) _____.

mundane (*adj.*)   of or relating to what is commonplace, ordinary,
,mən-'dān   or practical; **everyday**; **routine**

    14. The *mundane* details of everyday life often left Daryll feeling (excited, bored) _____.

overt (*adj.*)   open to view; **observable**; **evident**
ō-'vərt

15. When foreign troops (invaded, left) _____ the country, government officials called the event an *overt* act of war.

retract (*v.*)   take back or withdraw; **recant**; **disavow**
ri-'trakt

16. When the trucking supervisor found out about Doug's (theater, speeding) _____ tickets, she *retracted* her job offer.

stalwart (*adj.*)   characterized by strength and vigor; **unwavering**;
'stȯl-wərt   **resolute**; **steadfast**

17. *Stalwart* music fans (remained at, departed from) _____ the Woodstock concert during the heavy rain.

succulent (*adj.*)   full of juice; **juicy**; **tasty**
'sə-kyə-lənt

18. A hamburger is less likely to be *succulent* if it is (overdone, undercooked) _____.

verify (*v.*)   prove to be true, accurate, or real; **confirm**;
'ver-ə-fī   **substantiate**

19. Dr. Hull *verified* her conclusion on the basis of (facts, rumors) _____.

wistful (*adj.*)   full of yearning tinged with sadness; **longing**;
'wist-fəl   **melancholy**

20. With a *wistful* glance at his wife and baby, the soldier (arrived, left) _____ home.

SENTENCE COMPLETION 11–20: Enter the required lesson words from D, above.

1. After looking over her _____ for the upcoming European sales meetings, the manager asked her secretary to _____ the dates.

2. Expecting the meeting to waste half the day on a(n) _____ discussion of procedural details, workers greeted the consultant with _____ hostility.

3. Nothing provoked Ms. Zabrowski's _____ as much as having to listen to a doctor's incomprehensible medical _____.

4. Still on his vegetarian diet, Carlos gave a(n) _____ look at the _____ steak and took another helping of broccoli.

5. _____ supporters of the congressman demanded that the newspaper _____ its false accusations.

VOCABULARY IN CONTEXT 11–20: Read the paragraph, and on a separate sheet of paper, answer the questions that follow. Do not repeat any of the underlined words in your answers; use synonyms instead.

What is it about computer-knowledgeable people that makes them speak in technical <u>jargon</u>? Do these techies simply enjoy incurring the <u>ire</u> of nontechnical people who have no idea what the techies are talking about? Are the working details of computer use so <u>mundane</u> that techies must wrap them in mysterious <u>terminology</u>? Or do techies hide behind complicated language so that no one can <u>verify</u> the accuracy of their statements? I, for one, a <u>stalwart</u> *non*techie, would welcome some plain English for a change.

1. Paraphrase the paragraph.

2. Why do you think people in specialized fields, such as law and medicine, rely so heavily on jargon?

SYNONYMS: To avoid repetition, replace the boldfaced word with a synonym from the vocabulary list below.

evaluate	psychic	lacking	evident	juicy
melancholy	recant	confirm	unconventional	fair

1. Scurvy is a vitamin-deficiency disease that affects people whose diet is **deficient** in vitamin C.

    1. _____

2. The accused suspect tried to **retract** his confession, but it was too late for a retraction.

    2. _____

3. Florence will **assess** our business plan and then summarize her assessment in a written report.

    3. _____

4. Ralph's greatest eccentricity is his **eccentric** manner of dress.

    4. _____

5. Janis gazed wistfully into the distance, her broad-brimmed hat casting a shadow over her **wistful** expression.

    5. _____

6. Fortune-tellers say they are **clairvoyant**, but their predictions show little evidence of clairvoyance.

    6. _____

7. Although the editor **verified** all the facts in the article, there is some question about her method of verification.

    7. _____**ed**

8. The **succulent** chops are sizzling on the grill, their wonderful aroma a promise of their succulence.

    8. _____

9. The fielder was overtly angry with himself for having dropped the ball; he pounded his glove several times in a(n) **overt** sign of displeasure.

    9. _____

10. The border dispute was equitably resolved when the judge ordered a(n) **equitable** distribution of the property.

10. _____

H **ANTONYMS:** In the blank space in each sentence below, enter the word most nearly the antonym of the boldfaced word. Choose your antonyms from the following list.

---

disprove	weak	harmony	integrity	friendly
abundant	conventional	colorful	delight	dry

1. During her college days, Gina wore many **eccentric** outfits, but now she dresses only in _____ clothing.

2. People who have acquired a reputation for **duplicity** find it difficult to convince others of their _____.

3. The once **succulent** peach was now nothing more than a(n) _____ and shriveled memory.

4. In contrast to her **austere** appearance, Mrs. Fowler is actually one of the most _____ people in the building.

5. Weary of the **mundane** events of day-to-day living, Walter fantasized about having _____ adventures in faraway places.

6. The advancing army had expected only _____ resistance; instead, they encountered **stalwart** opposition.

7. Benjamin's memory my be **deficient** in historical facts, but it does contain a(n) _____ supply of sports statistics.

8. Reporters could not **verify** the boy's account of the flying saucer, but neither could they _____ it.

9. When Luisa learned that Chad's kindness had been nothing more than an act, her initial _____ vanished, and her eyes glowed with **ire**.

10. "It is time to put an end to **discord** in our community," said the mayor, "and work together to achieve greater _____."

| | **CONCISE WRITING:** Express the thought of each sentence in NO MORE THAN FOUR WORDS. |

---

1. The way in which Luke behaves is different from the usual way that people act.

   _____

2. Take back the words that you spoke accusing me, because they insult me!

   _____

3. The individuals doing detective work tried to determine the value and importance of the pieces of evidence.

   _____

4. I get confused by the specialized language used by people who are employed in the field of education.

   _____

5. Short sayings that are clever and convey wisdom are well worth remembering.

   _____

6. Individuals running for office place high value on the people who strongly and vigorously support them.

   _____

VOCABULARY SKILL BUILDER

Context Clues: Comparison and Contrast

Writers often compare or contrast people, places, or things. When writers *compare*, they focus on similarities; when they *contrast*, they highlight differences. Comparison-and-contrast context clues can help you figure out the meaning of unfamiliar words.

> *Example:* The situation at the office presented a <u>vexatious</u> problem, the kind that keeps you awake at night, like the relentless drip of a leaky faucet.

> *Context clues:* The writer compares the problem to the annoying "drip of a leaky faucet." This comparison suggests the meaning of *vexatious*—"causing irritation or annoyance."

> *Example:* The school board meeting, which had gotten off to such a quiet and orderly start, turned into <u>pandemonium</u> when Shari made her shocking proposal.

> *Context clues:* The writer contrasts the meeting's "quiet and orderly start" with the "pandemonium" that followed Shari's proposal. This contrast suggests the meaning of *pandemonium*—"wild uproar."

Exercises

1. On a separate sheet of paper, explain how comparison and contrast can help you understand the meaning of each underlined word. In exercise (b), circle a pair of antonyms.

   a. The actor arrived at the party dressed in the most <u>ostentatious</u> outfit anyone had ever seen. He looked like a peacock in a room full of ducks and geese.

   b. Emma is an eloquent speaker when among close friends, but she becomes <u>inarticulate</u> when she has to address a large group.

c. The award ceremony turned into an utter <u>fiasco</u> when Dr. Freynard refused to accept the prize. It was as though someone had thrown a surprise party and failed to invite the guest of honor.

2. A *simile* is a comparison using *like* or *as*. What similes can you identify in the above sentences?

 WRITING SKILL BUILDER

Developing Content: Comparison/Contrast

For some writing assignments, you need to compare or contrast people, places, or things. As you read in the preceding *Vocabulary Skill Builder*, comparison focuses on similarities, while contrast highlights differences.

Often, you will want to compare *and* contrast. For example, if you are writing an essay about two nations in the Middle East, you might begin by discussing how the two are alike and then discuss how they differ.

Activity

Choose two places that you have visited, such as restaurants, museums, or vacation destinations. Which of the two did you prefer? Why? Write an essay explaining—and supporting—your point of view. Use comparison and contrast to develop the content of your essay. Remember to include specific reasons, facts, details, or examples. In your writing, use at least two of the words that you have learned in this lesson. Write your essay on a separate sheet of paper.

LESSON 11

Lesson Preview

Some of the words that you will encounter on pages 124–126 and
127–128 of this lesson appear in bold type in the following poem.
Read the poem, and on a separate sheet of paper, answer the questions that follow.

> The reviews of the critics were cruel
> In expressing utter **disfavor**:
> "**Cancellation** would be merciful—
> This show doesn't have any flavor!"

> "The playwright tries to be **whimsical**,
> But the plot is banal and dreary,
> And the scenes that she **visualizes**
> Leave the audience bored and weary."

What is this poem about? Did the critics enjoy the show? Why or
why not?

 LESSON WORDS 1–10: Pronounce the word, spell it, study
its meanings, and finish the sentence that follows it.

---

accusation (*n.*)   charge of wrongdoing; **allegation**; **claim**
‚a-kyə-'zā-shən

    1. Based on *accusations* in the magazine article, it appears that
      the executive's stock trades may have been (legal, illegal)
      _____ .

brandish (*v.*)   shake or wave, usually in a threatening manner, as a
'bran-dish   weapon; **wield**; **flourish**

    2. As he approached his (friend, enemy) _____ , the
      warrior *brandished* his sword.

cancellation (*n.*)   act or instance of canceling or calling off;
,kan(t)-sə-'lā-shən   **termination; halt**

    3. (Weak, Strong) _____ ticket sales led to *cancellation* of the concert.

collaborate (*v.*)   work together with one or more other persons,
kə-'la-bə-,rāt   especially in a literary or scientific endeavor;
                  cooperate; team up

    4. Stephen King and Peter Straub have *collaborated* to (read, write) _____ best-selling novels.

contiguous (*adj.*)   in actual contact; **touching; adjacent**
kən-'ti-gyə-wəs

    5. (California, Hawaii) _____ is one of the 48 *contiguous* states.

disfavor (*n.*)   (1) unfavorable opinion; (2) state or fact of being
(,)dis-'fā-vər   regarded unfavorably; **disapproval; dislike**

    6. When the bold knight attempted to (kiss, help) _____ the princess, he fell into *disfavor* with the queen.

disparage (*v.*)   speak slightingly or critically about; **belittle;**
di-'spar-ij   **denigrate**

    7. *Disparaging* the skills of other athletes is a sign of (good, poor) _____ sportsmanship.

entrust (*v.*)   charge or invest with a trust or responsibility; put
in-'trəst   something in the care of; **trust; assign**

    8. Mrs. Morgan *entrusts* only her most (faithful, attractive) _____ employees with the combination to the safe.

flagrant (*adj.*)   conspicuously bad; **glaring; outrageous; blatant**
'flā-grənt

    9. The United Nations (praised, condemned) _____ several countries for their *flagrant* disregard of human rights.

inexorable (*adj.*)   unable to be persuaded, influenced, or stopped;
(,)i-'neks-rə-bəl   **relentless; inevitable; unyielding**

> 10. Troops loyal to the government were (able, unable)
> _____ to block the rebels' *inexorable* advance.

B | **SENTENCE COMPLETION 1–10:** Enter the required lesson words.

---

1. "I want to _____ you with a dark family secret," Alonzo told Catherine. "I hope that this information will not cause you to look upon me with _____."

2. Two architects _____**d** on this award-winning design of a series of _____ houses.

3. Although protesters tried to force the _____ of the project, they soon learned that its progress toward completion was

   _____.

4. "This is a(n) _____ violation of the city code," the building manager said, _____**ing** a handful of legal documents.

5. Justin resented the reporter's _____. "You have no right to _____ my accomplishments," he said.

 | **VOCABULARY IN CONTEXT 1–10:** Read the paragraph, and on a separate sheet of paper, answer the questions that follow. Do not repeat any of the underlined words in your answers; use synonyms instead.

Mrs. Knightly was shocked when she entered the restaurant. A large dog was asleep near the kitchen door.

"This is a <u>flagrant</u> violation of the health code," she informed the manager.

"I cannot deny your <u>accusation</u>," he replied. "However, my best friend <u>entrusted</u> me with the dog's care, and there is nowhere else for the animal to go. It is too cold to keep him outdoors."

"Aren't you concerned that customers will look upon the dog's presence with <u>disfavor</u>?"

"Actually," he answered, lowering his voice, "I'm more concerned that the dog may look upon the customers' presence with disfavor."

1. Summarize the conversation in your own words.

2. Reread the last sentence. Do you think the manager is joking? Why or why not?

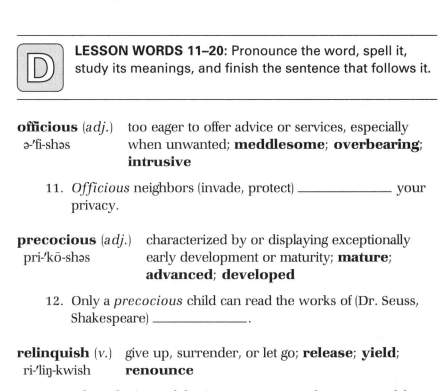

D **LESSON WORDS 11–20:** Pronounce the word, spell it, study its meanings, and finish the sentence that follows it.

---

officious (*adj.*)　too eager to offer advice or services, especially
ə-'fi-shəs　　　　when unwanted; **meddlesome**; **overbearing**;
　　　　　　　　intrusive

11. *Officious* neighbors (invade, protect) ＿＿＿＿＿＿ your privacy.

precocious (*adj.*)　characterized by or displaying exceptionally
pri-'kō-shəs　　　early development or maturity; **mature**;
　　　　　　　　advanced; **developed**

12. Only a *precocious* child can read the works of (Dr. Seuss, Shakespeare) ＿＿＿＿＿＿.

relinquish (*v.*)　give up, surrender, or let go; **release**; **yield**;
ri-'liŋ-kwish　　**renounce**

13. When she (gained, lost) ＿＿＿＿＿＿ the support of the people, the country's ruler agreed to *relinquish* her office.

saturate (*v.*)　fill, treat, or furnish with something to the point
'sa-chə-ˌrāt　　where no more can be absorbed or dissolved; **soak**;
　　　　　　　overfill

14. Our beach towels are *saturated* because we left them out in the (sun, rain) ＿＿＿＿＿＿.

sedentary (*adj.*)   doing or requiring much sitting; involving little
'se-d⁰n-,ter-ē   physical activity; **inactive**; **unmoving**

15. Telephone (operators, repairmen) _____ generally
have *sedentary* jobs.

stability (*n.*)   state or quality of being stable; strength to stand or
stə-'bi-lə-tē   remain; **firmness**; **steadiness**

16. The wooden stepladder in the garage is so (old, heavy)
_____ that I don't trust its *stability*.

surreptitious (*adj.*)   done or accomplished by stealth;
,sər-əp-'ti-shəs   **clandestine**; **secret**; **furtive**

17. The neighboring nations watched one another for (signs,
announcements) _____ of the *surreptitious* development of new weapons.

vigilant (*adj.*)   on guard; **watchful**; **alert**; **wary**
'vi-jə-lənt

18. The primary responsibility of a (messenger, sentry)
_____ is to remain *vigilant*.

visualize (*v.*)   form a mental image of; **envision**; **picture**
'vi-zhə-wə-,līz

19. Screenwriters must have (imagination, confidence)
_____ in order to *visualize* different scenes.

whimsical (*adj.*)   characterized by odd or fanciful notions; **playful**;
'hwim-zi-kəl   **curious**

20. Readers who enjoy *whimsical* literature should read (*Alice
in Wonderland, The World Almanac*) _____.

SENTENCE COMPLETION 11–20: Enter the required lesson words from D, above.

1. *The Phantom Tollbooth* is a(n) _____ novel in which the author _____ **s** all sorts of strange occurrences.

2. Government agents learned about the _____ meeting too late and feared that it might threaten the _____ of the regime.

3. Iris sometimes felt that her uncle was being _____, not helpful, and wished that he would _____ control of her life.

4. Louis was a(n) _____ boy, able to build complex aircraft models at the age of six, but he soon tired of such _____ activity.

5. "You must be _____," the chemist told her assistant. "Gradually add more salt to this solution, but do not allow the water to become _____**d** with it."

VOCABULARY IN CONTEXT 11–20: Read the paragraph, and on a separate sheet of paper, answer the questions that follow. Do not repeat any of the underlined words in your answers; use synonyms instead.

My friend Bruce is a night watchman at an office building in town. His job is to patrol the grounds every night, <u>vigilant</u> for any indications of wrongdoing. To me, this sounds like the most boring job in the world, but Bruce says he prefers it to sitting behind a desk every day. He's always hated <u>sedentary</u> jobs. Still, I find it hard to <u>visualize</u> being the only person in an empty office building at three o'clock in the morning, watching for signs of <u>surreptitious</u> activity. After a while, I think I'd begin to wonder about my mental <u>stability</u>.

1. Paraphrase the paragraph.

2. Are your own feelings closer to those of the narrator or Bruce? Why?

SYNONYMS: To avoid repetition, replace the boldfaced word with a synonym from the vocabulary list below.

allegation	termination	disapproval	belittle	glaring
playful	soak	watchful	picture	clandestine

1. When she felt stressed, Keira would **visualize** the tranquil beach where she had gone on vacation. It was such a relaxing visual image.

   1. _____

2. How could you have broken the rules so flagrantly? Didn't you realize that your behavior was a **flagrant** breach of conduct?

   2. _____

3. Please do not accuse Evan of disloyalty. He has done nothing to deserve such an **accusation**.

   3. _____

4. People who write children's books often have **whimsical** imaginations. Their books are filled with whimsy.

   4. _____

5. Mr. Corleone would greatly appreciate your doing him this favor as soon as possible. If you delay, you may incur his **disfavor**.

   5. _____

6. In her speech, the president declared that we must be ever **vigilant** in protecting our freedom. "Constant vigilance is every citizen's responsibility," she said.

   6. _____

7. Many people **disparaged** the director's work and spoke disparagingly of her latest film.

   7. _____d

8. The basement carpet is **saturated**! How could a slow drip from a leaky pipe cause the saturation of an entire carpet?

   8. _____ed

9. Club members gathered surreptitiously
at dawn, hoping that their
surreptitious meeting would not
arouse too much suspicion.   9. _____

10. I want to cancel my daily newspaper.
Will the **cancellation** of home
delivery require much time to process? 10. _____

H   **ANTONYMS:** In the blank space in each sentence below,
enter the word most nearly the antonym of the boldfaced
word. Choose your antonyms from the following list.

| isolated | praise | approval | avoidable | trivial |
| immature | retain | active | inattentive | direct |

1. "I shall never **relinquish** this castle," cried the duke. "I shall
_____ it by force if necessary!"

2. As a child, Kim was remarkably **precocious**, but as a teen, she
seems rather _____.

3. Oregon and Washington are **contiguous** states; Alaska, however, is _____.

4. After five **sedentary** months as a toll collector, Hector was hoping to find a more _____ job.

5. "I do not believe in **inexorable** fate," said the woman. "I think
that many of life's troubles are _____."

6. While the new candidate's proposals won widespread
_____, people viewed the present mayor with growing
disfavor.

7. The guards remained **vigilant** as long as they could, but as the
hours dragged on, they became increasingly _____.

8. Francisco **disparaged** mountain climbing as a sport for risk
takers, although he did _____ the courage of those who
tried it.

9. "Your criticism may not be a **flagrant** breach of etiquette," Robertson told his guest, "but it is far from a(n) _____ offense!"

10. Elana cast a **surreptitious** glance toward Mr. Dixon, afraid to make _____ eye contact.

| **CONCISE WRITING:** Express the thought of each sentence in NO MORE THAN FOUR WORDS.

---

1. The persons with whom Brenda shares a room are too eager to offer unwanted advice.

   _____

2. Earl makes untrue statements that go so far beyond all standards of what is right or decent that they are outrageous.

   _____

3. Do not charge anyone of wrongdoing if you know that your charges are not true.

   _____

4. The absorbent cloth that I use to dry myself is wet to the point where it cannot absorb any more water.

   _____

5. Make-believe witches and spiders and bats and other such objects used to decorate homes for Halloween are imaginative and playful.

   _____

6. The medieval soldiers in battle armor waved sharp steel weapons in a menacing way.

   _____

VOCABULARY SKILL BUILDER

Context Clues: Causes and Effects

A *cause* produces, or leads to, one or more *effects*—results or consequences. These effects may be direct or indirect. For instance, a lightning storm may cause a power failure, which in turn may cause traffic lights not to function, which may lead to car crashes.

Identifying causes and effects can help you determine the meaning of unfamiliar words.

> *Example:* Young Amy's comment was so <u>precocious</u> that several adults in the room expressed amazement. "So much insight for a child of only ten," said Mr. Morton admiringly.

> *Context clues:* The meaning of *precocious* in this context is suggested by the response of the other people in the room and Mr. Morton's remark. Amy's comment is the cause; the adults' reactions are the effects.

Exercises

On a separate sheet of paper, explain how cause and effect and your own knowledge and experience can help you infer the meaning of each underlined word.

1. "I'm afraid we're going to have to charge you for the missed appointment," said the receptionist. "The doctor requires 24 hour's notice for a <u>cancellation</u>, and you didn't call until early this afternoon."

2. Dad took one look at Kyle, scowled at the tattoos and piercings, and I knew that my new boyfriend had fallen into immediate <u>disfavor</u>.

3. Being a writer is one of the more <u>sedentary</u> occupations. Long hours of writing burn few if any calories, do nothing to develop physical fitness, and leave your entire body feeling stiff.

WRITING SKILL BUILDER

Developing Content: Cause and Effect

As you read in the preceding *Vocabulary Skill Builder*, a cause produces one or more effects, either directly or indirectly. For some writing assignments, you may want to organize or develop your content on the basis of cause and effect. For example, you might begin by describing an event and then discuss what factors led to that event or what consequences followed it.

Activity

Should schools devote more time to teaching students how to be wise consumers? Would more financial education better prepare students for the real world? Write an essay explaining your views on this question.

Use cause and effect to organize or develop your content. Remember to support your main ideas with specific reasons, facts, details, or examples. Use transitional words and phrases to connect ideas and supporting information. In your essay, use at least two of the words that you have learned in this lesson. Write your essay on a separate sheet of paper.

LESSON 12

Some of the words that you will encounter on pages 135–137 and 138–139 of this lesson appear in bold type in the following paragraph. Read the paragraph, and on a separate sheet of paper, answer the questions that follow.

> Participants at the writers' workshop take turns reading **excerpts** from their novels. After reading, the students discuss each work's **salient** features. Most of the criticism offered is gentle and constructive, though there are occasional **acerbic** remarks as well. One student often **enlivens** the meeting with hilarious anecdotes, and participants have to wait for the laughter to **subside** before discussion can continue.

Explain how context clues help you infer the meaning of each of the boldfaced words. What is the main idea of this paragraph?

 LESSON WORDS 1–10: Pronounce the word, spell it, study its meanings, and finish the sentence that follows it.

---

acerbic *(adj.)*   harsh or biting in mood, tone, or language; **sharp;**
ə-'sər-bik   **cutting; caustic**

   1. Delia's *acerbic* comments (upset, delighted) _____ her friends.

allegation *(n.)*   assertion not supported by proof; **accusation;**
ˌa-li-'gā-shən   **charge; claim**

   2. The witness provided (substantial, no) _____ evidence to support his *allegations* of criminal activity.

brevity (*n.*)   conciseness of expression; **shortness**; **briefness**
'bre-və-tē

    3. Despite its *brevity*, this (100, 1000) _____-page
       book contains many useful facts.

cite (*v.*)   (1) quote, as a passage or author, for the purpose of
'sīt   providing as an example, authority, or means of proof;
       name; **refer to** (2) call attention to as an example, proof,
       or precedent; **mention**; **bring up**

    4. The supervisor *cited* the employee's (excellent, poor)
       _____ performance record as grounds for promo-
       tion.

colleague (*n.*)   fellow worker; **associate**; **coworker**
'kä-(,)lēg

    5. One of my *colleagues* showed me how to use the (sports,
       office) _____ equipment.

dilapidated (*adj.*)   decayed or fallen into ruin, especially through
də-'la-pə-,dā-təd   neglect; **decrepit**; **run-down**

    6. The house on Long Drive sells for a (high, low)
       _____ price because it is so *dilapidated*.

enliven (*v.*)   make lively, active, or cheerful; add life to; **liven up**;
in-'lī-vən   **animate**

    7. Professor Steger *enlivens* his history lectures with occa-
       sional (jokes, statistics) _____.

excerpt (*n.*)   passage selected from a book, article, or other work;
ek-'sərpt   **extract**; **quotation**

    8. The magazine publisher told the reporter that if she wanted
       to include an *excerpt* in her story, she would need to get
       permission from the (author, editor) _____.

incur (*v.*)   become liable or subject to; bring on oneself; **invite**;
in-'kər   **acquire**

    9. The ancient Greeks tried not to (please, offend)
       _____ the gods because they did not want to *incur*
       their wrath.

levity (*n.*)   inappropriate or excessive lightness or gaiety in attitude
ˈle-və-tē   or behavior; lack of seriousness; **frivolity**; **flippancy**

10. When the children began to (giggle, write) _____,
the teacher scolded them for their *levity*.

B **SENTENCE COMPLETION 1–10**: Enter the required lesson words.

---

1. The department manager made _____**s** of improper computer use on the job against Kent and two of his _____**s**.

2. Your _____ wit may _____ the conversation, but it offends some people.

3. The Robinsons are sure to _____ huge expenses if they attempt to renovate that _____ house.

4. If your goal is _____, I suggest you choose a shorter _____ to include in your paper.

5. "_____**ing** the Constitution is no cause for _____," scolded the judge, when the attorney laughed.

C **VOCABULARY IN CONTEXT 1–10**: Read the paragraph, and on a separate sheet of paper, answer the questions that follow. Do not repeat any of the underlined words in your answers; use synonyms instead.

The movie reviewer <u>incurred</u> the anger of readers when he questioned the director's motives. Readers criticized the writer's <u>allegation</u> that the director was concerned "only with making bucks." They also objected to the reviewer's <u>acerbic</u> tone and demanded that he <u>cite</u> one piece of evidence supporting his claims. In response, the reviewer published an <u>excerpt</u> from an interview in which the director said that "one of my goals is to attain financial success."

1. What did the reviewer accuse the director of doing?

2. Do you think that the interview excerpt justifies the reviewer's allegation? Why or why not?

D **LESSON WORDS 11–20:** Pronounce the word, spell it, study its meanings, and finish the sentence that follows it.

---

menial (*adj.*)   suitable for a servant; **servile**; **low**; **unskilled**
mē-nē-əl

    11. Harrison had no interest in becoming a (butler, surgeon) _____ because he did not enjoy doing *menial* tasks.

notoriety (*n.*)   quality or state of being notorious, or widely but
‚nō-tə-'rī-ə-tē   unfavorably known; **disrepute**; **infamy**

    12. Through extensive media coverage, the couple gained *notoriety* as bank (tellers, robbers) _____ .

obsequious (*adj.*)   too eager to please, serve, or obey; **fawning**;
əb-'sē-kwē-əs   **toadying**

    13. The *obsequious* waiter (seldom, repeatedly) _____ returned to the movie star's table.

perfunctory (*adj.*)   done with little care or interest or merely as a
pər-'fəŋ(k)-tə-rē   routine; **superficial**; **indifferent**; **mechanical**

    14. The receptionist, (bored, delighted) _____ with her job, offered *perfunctory* greetings to visitors.

recourse (*n.*)   turning to someone or something for help or
'rē-‚kȯrs   protection, or the person or thing turned to; **resort**; **option**

    15. Considering your (symptoms, goals) _____, your best *recourse* is the health clinic.

salient (*adj.*)   standing out conspicuously; **prominent;**
'sā-lē-ənt   **outstanding**

16. (Red, Black) _____ hair is one of Jean's most
    salient features.

savory (*adj.*)   pleasing to the taste or smell; **palatable; appetizing**
'sā-və-rē

17. The chef's reputation for preparing *savory* dishes led to the
    restaurant's eventual (failure, success) _____ .

sequel (*n.*)   literary, cinematic, or televised work that is complete in
'sē-kwəl   itself but continues or extends a story started in a
    preceding work; **continuation; follow-up**

18. Readers were curious about the hero's (earlier, later)
    _____ adventures, so the author decided to write a
    sequel to her popular novel.

subside (*v.*)   become less active or intense; **abate; lessen;**
səb-'sīd   **decrease**

19. People hurried (to, from) _____ their shelters as
    soon as the storm *subsided*.

venerable (*adj.*)   deserving respect or reverence, as by reason of
've-nər(-ə)-bəl   age, character, or importance; **respected;**
    esteemed

20. A special celebration commemorated the long history of the
    venerable (university, supermarket) _____ .

E **SENTENCE COMPLETION 11–20:** Enter the required
lesson words from D, above.

---

1. Uninterested in such _____ tasks as washing and
   cleaning, Hazel made only a(n) _____ inspection of the
   building.

2. Although the politician had gained _____ for his outrageous comments, _____ followers were ready to do
anything he asked.

3. "Your best _____," said the queen's adviser, "is to seek
help from the _____ old wizard who lives in the village."

4. Once the initial excitement over the movie _____
_____**d**, people realized that the previous film was far
superior.

5. This _____ recipe is similar to yours, but there are a
number of _____ differences.

F **VOCABULARY IN CONTEXT 11–20:** Read the paragraph,
and on a separate sheet of paper, answer the questions
that follow. Do not repeat any of the underlined words in
your answers; use synonyms instead.

"A most unusual case," said the venerable doctor, shaking his
head. "Your most salient symptom appears to be an intense
desire for chocolate."

The young woman shrugged her shoulders and sighed. "I do
so enjoy a savory chocolate stew."

"Does your craving ever subside?" asked the physician.

"Only after I eat a large quantity of chocolate," she replied.

"Well, I guess your only recourse then may be to do exactly
that," said the doctor.

1. Summarize the conversation in your own words.

2. Do you think the doctor's response is a wise one? Why or why
not? What would you have suggested?

SYNONYMS: To avoid repetition, replace the boldfaced word with a synonym from the vocabulary list below.

animate	quotation	fawning	appetizing	superficial
respected	invite	infamy	accusation	name

1. The **savory** dish made Madeline's mouth water, as she paused to savor the delicious aroma.

   1. _____

2. Allowing such an incident to occur would **incur** the resentment of your neighbors.

   2. _____

3. The university's **allegation** is shocking. No one had expected administrators to allege that several students plagiarized materials.

   3. _____

4. Gregor's **obsequious** manner was meant to please Countess Roccolu, but the countess soon became impatient with her servant's obsequiousness.

   4. _____

5. The article excerpted two paragraphs from the former president's memoirs. The text was only a short **excerpt**, but it drew widespread reaction.

   5. _____

6. Celine livens up our meetings with her witty comments. When she doesn't attend, no one else seems capable of **enlivening** the discussion.

   6. _____**ing**

7. The inspector checked the package perfunctorily, too busy to do anything more than a **perfunctory** examination.

   7. _____

8. I think that your citation of Emerson is incorrect. I believe that you meant to **cite** Thoreau as the source of this quotation.

   8. _____

9. Even though the **venerable** old man
   had long been out of uniform, soldiers
   continued to venerate the general as
   though he were still a commanding
   officer.   9. _____

10. As the criminal's **notoriety** grew,
    law enforcement officers intensified
    their efforts to catch him, determined
    to put an end to his notorious activities. 10. _____

H **ANTONYMS:** In the blank space in each sentence below,
enter the word most nearly the antonym of the boldfaced
word. Choose your antonyms from the following list.

---

gravity	intensify	brand-new	dampen	unpalatable
insignificant	mild	wordiness	prequel	disreputable

1. When life's setbacks threaten to _____ your enthusiasm, look for some way to **enliven** your spirits.

2. How differently the two brothers turned out: one a **venerable**
   statesman, the other a(n) _____ rogue.

3. We had expected the committee's report to contain only
   _____ criticism, but instead it was filled with **acerbic**
   observations.

4. Public outrage concerning the proposal **subsided** for several
   days but then _____ **ed** again.

5. The _____ of their financial situation had company
   executives on edge; it was certainly not the time for **levity**.

6. The teacher polished the essay, eliminating its _____
   and creating a model of **brevity** for the class.

7. The **sequel** to the novel describes the hero's final days, while
   the _____ focuses on his childhood adventures in
   Indiana.

8. If you don't follow the recipe exactly, you'll turn my **savory** Ital-
   ian dish into a(n) _____ disaster!

9. The once shiny, _____ sports car was now a **dilapi-dated** wreck.

10. Reporters jotted down the **salient** points of the mayor's speech, omitting the _____ details.

CONCISE WRITING: Express the thought of each sentence in NO MORE THAN FOUR WORDS.

---

1. It did not take long for the angry feelings that John was experiencing to become less intense.

_____

2. Set down in writing the factual statements that stand out most.

_____

3. Plants with colorful petals add cheerfulness to a room.

_____

4. Legal professionals call attention to cases that are related as a means of establishing precedent.

_____

5. I declare to be untrue the assertions you have made that are not supported by any proof.

_____

6. The people with whom I work came here before the expected time.

_____

VOCABULARY SKILL BUILDER

Word Parts: Prefixes, Suffixes, and Roots

In Lessons 3, 4, and 8 (pages 30–31, 42, and 92), you learned the meaning of a number of prefixes, suffixes, and roots. Here are some others. The examples are vocabulary words or synonyms that appeared in this lesson or in a previous lesson.

Prefix	Meaning	Example
ad-	"to"	admonish
col-, com-, con-	"with" or "together"	collaborate
de-	"down," "away," or "from"	deviate
en-	"in" or "into"	enliven

Suffix	Meaning	Example
-fy	"make" or "cause to be"	mortify
-ity, -ty	"quality" or "condition"	stability

Root	Meaning	Example
tract	"pull" or "move"	retract
ver, vers, vert	"turn"	irreversible

Exercises

Each of the following words appears as a lesson word or a synonym in this lesson or in a previous lesson. Circle the prefixes and suffixes, and underline the roots, in these words. Then, on a separate sheet of paper, use each word in a sentence. You may use more than one word in the same sentence. If you need help, check a dictionary.

1. entrust
2. colleague
3. verify
4. detract
5. complexity

6. adverse
7. inadvertently
8. derive
9. levity
10. adept

WRITING SKILL BUILDER

Polishing Your Writing

Once you've put your ideas down on paper, reread what you have written and do whatever you can to improve it. For example, you may want to rearrange sentences, add more supporting details, or strengthen the final paragraph. Eliminate any clichés you spot, and replace passive constructions with active wording. Check your spelling and grammar. Make your writing as clear and effective as you can.

Activity

Find an editorial or letter to the editor in a newspaper or magazine that expresses a viewpoint with which you strongly *dis*agree. Write a persuasive essay presenting *your* views on the issue.

Support your main ideas with specific reasons, facts, details, or examples. Use transitional words and phrases to connect ideas and supporting information. In your essay, use at least two of the words that you have learned in this lesson.

Write two drafts of your essay. After you've completed your first draft, carefully evaluate what you have written. Then revise, edit, and proofread your work to create a polished second draft.

Unit III Review and Enrichment

CLOSE READING: Read the following statements. Then answer questions 1–10.

STATEMENTS

"I shall treasure this always," Cynthia told her parents, clutching the bracelet that had belonged to her great-grandmother.

The witness reluctantly nodded his head, indicating that he had indeed been part of the conspiracy.

"What a horrible movie," said Helen. "I found it utterly revolting from beginning to end."

Leroy had both the teacher and the students laughing for ten minutes when he told the story about the dog running away with his cell phone.

Winston refuses to wear socks or shoes that match because he says he prefers to display a style of his own.

The players remained in the dugout for nearly an hour, wondering whether the rain would ever stop so that the baseball game could begin.

Strangely enough, when Tamar gets a feeling that someone she knows is about to call, she's usually right.

"I'll tell you exactly what to do," said Hilde for about the hundredth time. "Just listen to me. My advice is solid as a rock. Are you listening? I'll tell you exactly what to do. Are you listening?"

The company president selected Mr. Altman to be his representative at the conference in New Orleans.

"I'll bet that *you're* the one who ate my cookie," Ben said to his sister. "I can see chocolate on your face!"

QUESTIONS

1. Who is eccentric?_____

2. Who made a tacit admission? _____

3. Who enlivened the class?_____

4. Who was designated? _____

5. Who made an accusation? _____

6. Who saw something lurid? _____

7. Who waited for something to subside?_____

8. Who appears to be clairvoyant? _____

9. Who received an heirloom? _____

10. Who was officious? _____

B   **CONCISE WRITING:** Make the following passages more concise using no more than the number of words suggested.

---

1. The child who displayed exceptionally early maturity amazed everyone by showing that she could understand the specialized language of computer use. *(Cut to about 11–15 words.)*

---

2. The fact that the factory closed down was a disastrous event that caused great hardship for the workers in the town who earned wages, leaving the workers' families with few options for seeking assistance. *(Cut to about 19–23 words.)*

---

3. "This courtroom of mine is no place for remarks that do not show proper respect or seriousness," the judge said in a scolding way. "Any further display of inappropriate gaiety in the way people behave, and I will make every person leave the room!" *(Cut to about 20–24 words.)*

_____

_____

4. The first city that is listed in the proposed route of the trip that the Harmons are planning to take is known by many people for its churches that are esteemed for their age and importance. *(Cut to about 14–17 words.)*

_____

5. The people with whom Marvin works look upon him with an unfavorable opinion because of the deceitful way he has acted in the past. *(Cut to about 12–15 words.)*

_____

 CLOSE READING: Read the following statements. Then answer questions 11–20.

STATEMENTS

Although the publisher offered to provide a cowriter, the actress said that she preferred to write her autobiography without assistance.

"The last Harry Potter book was wonderful," said Jill. "I can't wait to read the next one."

The sailor in the crow's nest peered into the distance, on the lookout for any signs of approaching pirate ships.

"We will never surrender in our quest for liberty," cried the rebel leader. "We will fight to the bitter end!"

"As Shakespeare wrote in *Julius Caesar*," Professor Hull told the class, "'cowards die many times before their deaths.'"

The historian carefully examined the document before finally concluding that it was genuine.

Francine regretted her outburst. "I take it back," she said. "I didn't really mean to criticize you."

As soon as the ball crashed through his living room window, Mr. Wilson came running out of the house, face bright red with anger as he began yelling at the boys.

"If only I could win the lottery," thought Bonnie. "I'd movie into an enormous mansion with a gorgeous swimming pool and a spectacular flower garden."

"Six-gun Sam" soon became known throughout the West, and his picture appeared on numerous Wanted posters.

QUESTIONS

11. Who is eager for a sequel?_____

12. Who cited words? _____

13. Who displayed ire? _____

14. Who verified something? _____

15. Who was vigilant?_____

16. Who was belligerent? _____

17. Who visualized a scene?_____

18. Who retracted words? _____

19. Who did not want to collaborate? _____

20. Who gained notoriety? _____

ANALOGIES: Which lettered pair of words—a, b, c, d, or e—most nearly has the same relationship as the numbered pair? Enter the letter of your answer in the space provided.

1. OFFICIOUS : MEDDLE
   a. deficient : provide   b. sympathetic : care
   c. stalwart : instruct   d. precocious : animate
   e. obsequious : disparage   1. _____

2. LURID : SHOCK
   a. eager : brevity   b. belligerent : compromise
   c. imaginative : duplicity   d. flippant : respect
   e. comical : amusement   2. _____

3. RETAIN : RELINQUISH
   a. visualize : envision   b. depict : create
   c. incur : acquire   d. terminate : begin
   e. harangue : educate   3. _____

4. WATCH : VIGILANT
   a. perceive : clairvoyant   b. respect : venerable
   c. exasperate : angry   d. subside : intense
   e. assess : whimsical   4. _____

5. DILAPIDATED : DECREPIT
   a. banal : varied   b. original : salient
   c. wistful : longing   d. tacit : explicit
   e. ancient : fragile   5. _____

VOCABULARY SKILL BUILDER

Do the following exercises on a separate sheet of paper.

1. Explain how the connotation of a word differs from the denotation. Then list four pairs of synonyms in which one of the words has a positive or favorable connotation and the other has a negative or unfavorable connotation.

2. Explain how context clues can help you figure out the meaning of each underlined word.

   a. When he was young, Antonio had a belligerent attitude. As he got older, however, he learned to get along with people through negotiation and compromise.

   b. Candidates who make promises but then fail to keep them after being elected are sure to incur the ire of voters.

   c. The brevity of Martha's speech was a welcome relief after the endless babbling of the previous speakers.

3. Circle the prefixes and suffixes, and underline the roots, in these words. Then use each word in a sentence. You may use more than one word in the same sentence. If you need help, check a dictionary.

   a. convert   b. adversity   c. contract

4. Write the meaning of each of the following word parts, and give an example of a word containing each one. Then use each of your words in a sentence.

   de-   en-   -fy   -ity   tract

Cumulative Review for Units I, II, and III

A Circle the word that best completes each sentence.

1. Because Rachel often makes up stories, people cannot rely on her _____.

   a. apparition   b. acumen   c. veracity   d. temerity

2. The _____ note frustrated Isaac, who could not figure out who had sent it or exactly what it meant.

   a. zealous   b. affable   c. mundane   d. cryptic

3. "Stop and think before you take action," Dad advised. "Don't be so _____."

   a. whimsical   b. obsequious   c. impetuous   d. wistful

4. Negotiations reached a(n) _____ despite the fact that both sides were making a sincere effort to resolve the dispute.

   a. impasse   b. interim   c. anecdote   d. itinerary

5. Even though the charges were shown to be false, the gossip surrounding them has done _____ damage to my reputation.

   a. irreparable   b. inimitable   c. frenetic   d. parsimonious

6. People who _____ to be movie stars usually have to settle for less glamorous careers.

   a. discern   b. aspire   c. derive   d. succumb

7. The product advertised on the Internet did not actually work; the offer was nothing more than a _____.

   a. hoax   b. penchant   c. forte   d. valise

8. The general planned a _____ operation in which soldiers would sneak into the village before dawn.

   a. poignant   b. banal   c. clandestine   d. torrid

9. A fallen tree blocked the road to town, so we had to take a
   _____ route.
   a. flippant   b. menial   c. flagrant   d. circuitous

10. In order to devise a satisfactory solution, you must first carefully
   _____ the problem.
   a. espouse   b. extricate   c. relinquish   d. assess

B Circle the correct synonym for each underlined word.

11. squalid living conditions
   a. foul   b. mandatory   c. exuberant   d. just

12. ambiguous feelings
   a. periodic   b. discreditable   c. peevish   d. conflicted

13. obsequious behavior
   a. fawning   b. aggressive   c. sinister   d. fallacious

14. brandish a weapon
   a. distinguish   b. involve   c. wield   d. remove

15. alleviate your concerns
   a. evade   b. debilitate   c. lessen   d. animate

16. the intricacy of a plot
   a. discretion   b. complexity   c. development   d. reparation

17. designate a representative
   a. hamper   b. denounce   c. appoint   d. evaluate

18. a significant modification
   a. adjustment   b. consolation   c. ploy   d. incursion

19. an eccentric writer
   a. industrious   b. abstruse   c. impoverished
   d. unconventional

20. facilitate a plan
   a. impede   b. aid   c. reconcile   d. explicate

Vocabulary Index

bold type = lesson word; light type = synonym

Pronunciation Symbols

The system of indicating pronunciation is used by permission. From *Merriam-Webster's Collegiate Dictionary*, Tenth Edition, © 1993 by Merriam-Webster, Incorporated.

ə	banana, collide, abut
'ə, ˌə	humdrum, abut
ᵊ	immediately preceding \l\, \n\, \m\, \ŋ\, as in battle, mitten, eaten, and sometimes cap and bells \-ᵊm-\ lock and key \-ᵊŋ-\; immediately following \l\, \m\, \r\, as often in French table, prisme, titre
ər	operation, further, urger
'ər- 'ə-r	as in two different pronunciations of hurry \'hər-ē, 'hə-rē\
a	mat, map, mad, gag, snap, patch
ā	day, fade, date, aorta, drape, cape
ä	bother, cot, and, with most American speakers, father, cart
à	father as pronounced by speakers who do not rhyme it with bother
aủ	now, loud, out
b	baby, rib
ch	chin, nature \'nā-chər\ (actually, this sound is \t\ + \sh\)
d	did, adder
e	bet, bed, peck
'ē, ˌē	beat, nosebleed, evenly, easy
ē	easy, mealy
f	fifty, cuff
g	go, big, gift
h	hat, ahead
hw	whale as pronounced by those who do not have the same pronunciation for both *whale* and *wail*
i	tip, banish, active
ī	site, side, buy, tripe (actually, this sound is \ä\ + \i\, or \à\ + \i\)

j   **j**ob, **g**em, e**dg**e, **j**oin, **j**u**dg**e (actually, this sound is \d\ + \zh\)

k   **k**in, **c**ook, a**ch**e

k̲   German i**ch**, Bu**ch**

l   **l**i**l**y, poo**l**

m   **m**ur**m**ur, di**m**, ny**m**ph

n   **n**o, ow**n**

ⁿ   indicates that a preceding vowel or diphthong is pronounced with the nasal passages open, as in French *un bon vin blanc* \oeⁿ-bȯⁿ-vaⁿ-bläⁿ\

ŋ   si**ng** \'siŋ\, si**ng**er \'siŋ-ər\, fi**ng**er \'fiŋ-gər\, i**n**k \'iŋk\

ō   b**o**ne, kn**ow**, b**eau**

ȯ   s**aw**, **a**ll, gn**aw**

œ   French b**oeu**f, German H**ö**lle

œ̄   French f**eu**, German H**öh**le

ȯi   c**oi**n, destr**oy**, saw**i**ng

p   **p**e**pp**er, li**p**

r   **r**ed, ca**r**, **r**a**r**ity

s   **s**ource, le**ss**

sh   with nothing between, as in **sh**y, mi**ss**ion, ma**ch**ine, spe**ci**al (actually, this is a single sound, not two); with a hyphen between, two sounds as in death's-head \'deths-ˌhed\

t   **t**ie, a**tt**ack

th   with nothing between, as in **th**in, e**th**er (actually, this is a single sound, not two); with a hyphen between, two sounds as in knigh**th**ood \'nīt-ˌhu̇d\

t̲h̲   **th**en, ei**th**er, **th**is (actually, this is a single sound, not two)

ü   r**u**le, y**ou**th, uni**o**n \'yün-yən\, few \'fyü\

u̇   p**u**ll, w**oo**d, b**oo**k, curable \'kyu̇r-ə-bəl\

ue   German f**ü**llen, h**ü**bsch

u̅e̅   French r**ue**, German f**üh**len

v   **v**i**v**id, gi**v**e

w   **w**e, a**w**ay; in some words having final \(ˌ)ō\ a variant \ə-w\ occurs before vowels, as in \'fäl-ə-wiŋ\, covered by the variant \ə(-w)\ at the entry word

y   **y**ard, **y**oung, cue \\'ky**ü**\\, union \\'y**ü**n-yən\\

ʸ   indicates that during the articulation of the sound represented by the preceding character the front of the tongue has substantially the position it has for the articulation of the first sound of *yard*, as in French *digne* \\dēnʸ\\

yü   **you**th, **u**nion, **cu**e, f**ew**, m**u**te

yu̇   c**u**rable, f**u**ry

z   **z**one, rai**s**e

zh   with nothing between, as in vi**si**on, a**z**ure \\'a**zh**-ər\\ (actually, this is a single sound, not two); with a hyphen between, two sounds as in ga**zeh**ound \\'gāz-ˌhau̇nd\\

\\   slant line used in pairs to mark the beginning and end of a transcription: \\'pen\\

ˈ   mark preceding a syllable with primary (strongest) stress: \\'-pen-mən-ˌship\\

ˌ   mark preceding a syllable with secondary (next-strongest) stress: \\'pen-mən-ˌship\\

-    mark of syllable division

( )   indicate that what is symbolized between is present in some utterances but not in others: *factory* \\'fak-t(ə)rē\\